Results Press
Unit 229
#180, 8601 Lincoln Blvd.
Los Angeles, California
90045

www.theresultspress.com

ISBN-13: 978-0-9988905-6-2

First Edition

Copyright © 2020 by Sherry Turuk

All rights reserved. No part of this book may be reproduced in any form without the prior writer permission from the publisher. The opinions and conclusions drawn in this book are solely those of the author. The author and publisher bear no liability in connection with the use of the ideas presented.

This Book is Dedicated to Our Boy Mason!

The reason I chose this path in my life at this time is because of our dogs Mason and Brady. Mason was full of life and made us laugh every day because of his antics. People still ask us about Mason or share funny stories about him.

He has now passed but we dearly miss him.

I think of all the dogs that have come and gone over the years and what each one has taught me. I am forever grateful!

Speak Dog

INTRODUCTION

Our dogs are living in a state of confusion, but no one sees it or understands what we are doing to the dog. Worst of all, instead of learning how to correct the problem, most people ignore it until the dog is older and something serious happens that we created.

I tried everything with my dogs Mason and Brady, and yet I didn't understand I wasn't speaking to the dogs in the manner in which they understood. I had bags of treats, whistles, clickers and every available book on dog training, and yet if I went anywhere with my dogs, I couldn't get them to come back to me. I'd like a madwoman, cry and bribe the dogs. Everyone I knew would gladly give me words of advice, which was appreciated but didn't work. I'd have to call my husband to help me find the dogs yet again.

I was going crazy! I'd come home only to become frustrated when my husband would say one word to the dogs, and they'd respond immediately. He could walk the dogs off-leash and they'd never run away. He was the leader. I, however, was not! My dogs knew it, I knew it, yet I didn't understand how important body language was for a dog, so I couldn't correct the problem.

I thought I had to be mad or serious with my dogs (bad energy). I was stressed all the time when I was out with the dogs. I was feeding them a food that was of no interest or value for them (bad nutrition). They enjoyed the high value treats such as cheese (*so* bad for your dog's health) or peanut butter. I was creating monsters with treats! I thought I was doing so well when I would as my dog to sit while in the house and they would properly respond. I'd give them a treat. Then I would go out for a walk and take comfort in the treats I carried along, but then the bunny chase was so much more fun than the treat in my hand.

I'd go crazy when anyone would come to the door and would block the dogs so they wouldn't bolt (lack of mental stimulation). They constantly demanded attention from people, whether the person wanted to be around the dogs or not. They'd Jump and lick faces. Some people love that, but most don't, so I'd be so embarrassed. I would try to put them in a crate, and they would shiver as if they were scared(manipulation), so I would let them out.

Then Mason decided he was going to chase cars. The problems just got worse and worse the older the dogs got. I didn't understand the importance of training them at a young age. **I didn't understand that you start small and build on what you're teaching your dog. Only advance when the dog is ready to learn more.** It's important to continue the mental challenges and feed your dog a quality, species-appropriate food. Socialization is a big part of a dog's life, as well, letting your dog be a dog, to run, sniff and play with other dogs.

Over the years, this has all come together for me, so I am now going to share what I know with you!

Some of the names of humans/dogs and identifying details have been changed to protect the privacy of individuals.

Outline

Chapter 1 - STOP DOING WHAT YOU ARE DOING
Chapter 2 - NAUGHTY DOG
Chapter 3 - BECOMING THE EXPERT
Chapter 4 - IT'S NOT WHAT YOU THINK
Chapter 5 – THE PAST IS IRRELEVANT
Chapter 6 - WHO MAKES THE RULES — MANIPULATION 101
Chapter 7 - DON'T ASK
Chapter 8 – CHANGE — NO. CONSISTENCY — YES!
Chapter 9 - FOOD MATTERS
Chapter 10 - CONFIDENT MANAGER
Chapter 11 - SCARED STIFF
Chapter 12 - QUIT APOLOGIZING
Chapter 13 - CLEVER K9
Chapter 14 - TRAIN DAILY
Chapter 15 - PARTY TIME!
Chapter 16 - IN THE HABIT OF GETTING ATTENTION
Chapter 17 - A DOG'S TALE
Chapter 18 - GOOD CLEAN FUN
Chapter 19 - BE A SMART FIGHTER
Chapter 20 - CONCLUSION — MY STORY

CHAPTER 1

Stop Doing What You are Doing

We talk to dogs, we move for dogs, we carry dogs, we hand feed dogs, we let the dog ride on our laps while we're driving, we let the dog run out the front door in front of us, we let the dog trip us on stairs, we yell at our dogs, we let the dog jump all over grandma, we let the dog pee and poop in our homes, we let the dog chew up all our shoes, we let the dog use our kids as chew toys, we let the dog bark at anything, we let the dog drag us down the street on our walks. I am sure you could list many more issues that start with the words "We let…"

The reason I say, "We let" is only because we don't understand how what we're doing indicates to the dog that they're doing the exact behaviour we want them to do. From the time we bring our new family member home, "We let" the dog do all of the things I listed above. By the time the dog is eight months old, we're screaming for help.

If you brought your dog home from a shelter, these things may start to occur within two months. Most people don't even identify that this is what's happening until I point it out. The dog is so cute. Don't you just love him/her/my baby? I'll start training when they're a year old.

Yet by doing this, we are unintentionally setting the dog up for failure. When the dog is one-to-three years old, all of a sudden, their already-learned actions are bad behaviour and the dog is driving the owners crazy. Everyone needs to think about what they're doing from the time you walk in the front door with your new family member. I love it when people hire me even before they bring the dog home.

This is what I suggest you consider. Don't blame the dog. Rather, look at what you are doing and how, from a dog's perspective, they may be confused. I will guarantee it will make sense when I help you understand how a dog speaks to us.

Dogs don't pay attention to words, but they do pay attention to body language in humans and dogs. That's how a dog gathers its information about everything going on in his world. From the time you bring that pup home, he is gathering information about you and your family. He doesn't know you. He only sees how you react to everything he does.

You bend over, you pick him up, you laugh when he bites you, you talk to him constantly, you clean up his pee and you take him into your bed.

I want you to stop and think about just a few days before you brought the pup home. The pup was with his mom and siblings. How do you think the mother would have handled all of these situations? I know for sure she would not have been talking to the pup and she wouldn't cater to the pup. If the pup nipped or bit Mom too hard, she would have corrected the pup. Mom and pups would sleep in their bed on the floor.

Now suddenly you bring the pup home, carry him into the house, talk constantly, put him in your bed, and within a short period of time, your pup is confused! Confusion is the root of all evil. Clear up the confusion, be consistent, have expectations and *teach*, don't *react*! Reactions are always bad and are done wrong. Teaching is about setting up your dog for success and helping the dog to learn. The mom would teach, and her message would be clear. She wouldn't second guess what she was doing. She'd make quick, confident decisions. She is a confident leader, whereas we tend to second guess everything we do with the dog. Are we feeding the right amount at the right time of day? Where should the pup sleep? How much time do they need to spend outdoors? I think they may need more toys.

Every time we change our minds or change what we're doing, the puppy becomes confused. They didn't live in that environment prior to coming into our homes. Even if you bring a shelter dog home, as long as you're clear about your expectations, the dog will jump on board and see you understand dogs. Dogs like to please and follow, so be a good leader for them! That's all they expect from us. But if we don't lead, they will, and this is where the problems come in.

Vanessa and Slick

I had a young girl in my group class. She'd brought her pup out to attend my dog training program and hopefully get some socialization for the pup. This particular program was six weeks long, meeting twice a week for an hour. From Lesson One right until the end, her pup was on board with everything we did. I appreciated the fact that she enjoyed the lessons and had such great results.

At the beginning of Week Three, several of my clients were struggling with the concepts, not doing the homework, always talking to their dogs, and expecting that those two one-hour classes a week would train their dogs. However, this young girl was having huge success, so I continued to challenge her to challenge her dog. She was successful no matter what I asked her to do. At one point, she was at least 25' from her dog and the dog maintained a *SIT* and *STAY*. I stopped the class and asked everyone to observe. I ask the rest of my clients why she could be at such a distance from her dog and why the dog remained in a *SIT/STAY* at that distance? Most everyone decided it was because the pup was a border collie — you know, because they are the smart ones. So I ask her to grab any other dog in class. I held her dog and off she went. She didn't ask, she just grabbed a leash from another dog owner and walked off with the dog. The dog followed. Then she put the dog in a *SIT*. She moved around for a bit and went back to give the dog a pat. Within no time, the dog was 25' away from her and sitting.

This young girl was so strong and confident! She knew how to handle a leash, she moved with speed and purpose and she was always calm. Almost all dogs respond to this type of leader. It had nothing to do with her having a border collie and everything to do with her being a calm, strong, confident leader.

Be that leader for your dog!

Denise, Family and Puppy

I had a couple who contacted me a few weeks after they brought their pup home. They attended one of my private lessons to see if they agreed with my training techniques and quickly decided my program would work for them. I gave them a few tips to help them until we started the training session. Crate-train the pup, sit on the floor when playing with the pup, don't talk too much to the pup, let the pup have all four paws on the floor at all times, and then we went through some potty training tips.

This couple had two children and were first-time dog owners. Having a puppy can be demanding at best, and yet here they were, first time dog owners with children, and both the adults had careers. Attending class and adding that much distraction made the training more difficult, but the pup did very well. As the training session went along, I helped this couple fine tune a few of their actions. When they walked, they'd always turn and look at the dog. They were not talking to their pup a lot, but I asked them not to talk to the dog at all for a while. The whole family would take part in the training classes.

By the time, this pup was eight months old, the owners would go running every morning and the pup would run between the two of them. Here is another example of calm, confident leaders. This couple took everything they'd learned and applied the homework. This couple understood the importance of meeting your dog's physical, mental, social, and nutritional needs. When they ran with the dog, they were moving with speed and purpose. The family had friends with a pup, so they'd let the dogs play. The family attended obedience classes to mentally stimulate the pup, and he was fed a quality raw food product to meet his nutritional needs. I still see this couple out running with their dog, and he is never on a leash. That is a win, for sure!

How would you like to trust your dog so much that you'd never have the dog on a leash?

Emily and Nick

A young girl contacted me to register for a group class. She had rescued a large dog from the local shelter. When she arrived on the first night, the dog was sitting on the seat next to her in the car. When she got out of the car, the dog dragged her to the area where I was setting up for class. She had no control over the dog.

The dog slept in her bed and was peeing in the house, and her idea of a quality life for the dog was cuddling on the couch or her bed. Anytime someone would get close to her, the dog would lunge to the end of the leash, dragging her along. The dog would get so close it would make contact with its mouth but not was not yet biting. She would wrap the leash around her hand, place the dog in a SIT and tell the dog not to be scared while she was rubbing or patting the dog. Her mother attended the classes with her. They were concerned about the dog's behaviour and had decided that he had been abused and that is why he was behaving in this manner. They felt sorry for the dog, so instead of having rules, expectations, and consistency with him, they catered to him in hopes he'd understanding they cared for him and therefore the dog didn't need to react.

I love that people care so much, but everything they were doing confirmed to the dog that it had a perfectly good reason to react the way it was, so the behaviour only got worse. This young girl was terrified because she didn't have the strength to control the dog and never would, so she began to just stay home instead of teaching the dog and exposing him to new environments. Everything she did was adding to the state of confusion this dog was feeling.

In this scenario, everything that could go wrong did go wrong, and the dog eventually ended up back in the shelter. First of all, the girl felt sorry for the dog. Dogs do not understand that you feel sorry for them. They just react to your energy. If you have bad energy, they will respond to that. Secondly, she took a dog home that in no way could she physically manage, and she had no experience as a dog owner to help this dog even if it did have some issues that needed work. She would wrap the leash in her hand, which told the dog they would be constantly encountering problems. She was nervous every time she took the dog out, so that stressed the dog. The dog was allowed to be at her level instead of her going down to the dog's level. The dog viewed her as an equal — or worse yet, as lower than the dog. She allowed the dog to come into her home and crawl in her bed. Again, now she is lower than the dog. Not any of the dog's needs were met — physical, mental, social, or nutritional. Only hers. She was anxious and stressed and she would use the dog to calm her down by petting and cuddling with him.

There is nothing wrong with all of these things but teach a dog first. If you are stressed all the time, your dog will react. This girl most likely did need a therapy dog but bringing home a dog from a shelter does not necessarily qualify as a therapy dog. This dog came into her home and quickly learned it needed to be the leader and took over that role. She continued to come to class but would not do any of the exercises and didn't apply any of the rules for the dog to learn. By week three she realized how much work training a dog could be and quit coming. As I said earlier, the dog ended up back in the shelter.

Conclusion

So DO be a strong, confident leader. This is what a dog needs until it understands its place in the pack, your family. It is very important for you to stand tall, move with speed and purpose, feed a quality dog food, have rules and expectations, provide the physical, mental, social and nutritional needs for your dog, allow your dog to have all four paws on the floor, provide him with its space (their own bed, not yours) and limit your talking.

Your dog needs and wants you to be a leader, so be that leader for your dog. This is what you signed up for when you decided to be a dog owner. There are some really good dogs and some not so good dogs, but at the end of the day, it is your job to teach. If you aren't willing to teach, it isn't the dog's fault. I haven't seen a dog yet that won't respond to a calm, confident leader.

Action Plan:
1) Be a confident leader!
2) Stand tall, shoulders back, chest out.
3) Take five deep breaths. Be calm.
4) It's the dog's job to watch you, not your job to watch the dog.
5) Teach, don't react.
6) Be consistent with your expectations.
7) Four on the floor. The dog must have four paws on the floor at all times.
8) You need your space and the dog needs its space. Train your dog to be happy in a kennel.
9) Drag a leash on the dog. This is the only way you can control the dog without rewarding it with touch. When the pup is doing something wrong, you grab the leash and walk away instead of reacting and grabbing the dog. The dragging leash must only be attached to the dog when you are indoors teaching your dog.
10) Buy a martingale collar and a 6' leash.

Measure of Success
    What does your body language look like? Are you confident? Are you creating a calm environment? Are you ready to teach?

CHAPTER 2

Naughty Dog

Dog owners try every possible method out there to train their dog, but so many don't work. As my time as a dog trainer and dog owner continued, I began to think back to when I was a child. Our family had a few dogs. I reflected on how we treated our dogs. They were never in the house. They ate the family's supper leftovers. We didn't spend any time training the dogs, and yet, we lived right along a major highway and our dogs never roamed. Many of my clients were farmers and ranchers. When I visited their homes, I realized what we do today with our dogs is quite different and doesn't always work. We need to adjust a few things to make our new family member happy.

When we bring our dogs into our homes, we leave food lying around and they suffer from lack of exercise, lack of mental stimulation and a lack of quality nutrition.

Now, I'm not saying all of this is bad, but I will explain why this makes such a difference in our dogs and the way these "naughty dogs" behave today.

First of all, we may be bringing our new pup into a home full of stress, yelling and screaming, loud music and children running around with high-pitched noise. Most dog owners may think leaving music or the TV on while they are away may comfort their dog, but I have seen more than enough times where this creates additional stress for the dog. Over time, your dog may become accustomed to all the activity and noise, but it may not. If you want a calm dog, you must provide the dog with a calm life.

Second, years ago, many dogs had to find their own food. They would wander around looking for food — a mouse, rabbit, etc. Dogs would spend hours searching for food. When you let your dog off leash, watch what they are doing — sniffing and smelling as they search for food. This is constructive work for a dog. We get grossed out when our dogs eating mice, rabbits, or fish, but they love it and even roll in it. Then, the dog will run and chase the food they need.

Sometimes they will eat grass. We tend to leave food lying around the house for the dog to eat whenever he desires. Again we are catering to the dog and not making the dog work for his food. Remember, the dog only goes by what is visual to them. If we set their food down and allow them a few minutes to eat, we are giving them food and then taking their food away. We're providing for the dog, which they interpret as us being the leader or doing what mom used to do before they left the litter. Even so, your dog needs to be let off the leash to wander, sniff and search. Maybe they'll find a mouse or two as a snack, reward for a job well done.

Third is a lack of exercise. A dog's natural movement is to walk or run. They come from times or places when they were allowed to roam with no collars or leashes. Dogs would roam from morning to night and sleep in the hottest part of the day or at night. Something that is so natural and good for their dog ends up being the last thing on an owner's to-do list. Movement is a critical part of mental and physical health for your dog. Movement relieves stress, allows the food in their body's to digest properly which can release toxins and allows the dog to explore, which is a big part of their social lives. Again, I would like you to pay attention to your dog when he is running off leash. Notice how often they pee and poop. Natural movement helps to aid in your dog's ability to release food and toxins from their body. You may use your dog as a "therapy dog," but he still needs to run to release the stress you are putting on him. A dog in a home with lots of noise needs to run to release the stress he gathers from the home.

Fourth is the lack of mental stimulation. We tend to have no expectations for the dog's behaviour. We are not consistent. We don't teach the dog to make good decisions and we put up with all the bad bullying behaviour he may do. If we don't give our dogs something good to do, such as a *SIT*,

STAY, DOWN or COME, they will make their own decisions about what they should do. You likely won't be happy with their decisions, which may include chewing shoes, bolting out of doors, jumping, barking, digging. This is how the dog expresses their lack of mental stimulation. I get told daily how smart a dog is. Well, put those brains to work on some solid constructive exercises that will make your pup the best companion dog you have ever owned.

Fifth is a lack of quality nutrition. Dogs need a species-appropriate diet! Dogs still carry 98.8% of their DNA from their ancestors. This is why a species-appropriate diet is so important for mental and physical health. Every one of us knows when you eat clean, whole, living or raw food over processed food, you look and feel better. Not only does your physical health improve, but your mental health is better because you are taking care of yourself and your body the way you should.

Dogs don't have a choice. They have to eat whatever you put in front of them. It is your decision if you choose to eat unhealthy food but your dog does not have a choice. Feed him food that will allow him to be healthy and vibrant.

As you can see, all these things may not be working well for our companions. When you put all these issues together, dogs may not behave the way we expect to and then we have a hard time trying to figure out what's wrong and how we can fix it. Physical, mental, social, and nutritional issues are incredibly important for the health and wellbeing of your dog.

Michelle and Blue

Years ago I had a young woman call me crying over the phone. I agreed to meet with her to see what was happening between her and her dog. She had rescued a dog, a female around two years old. She got the dog spayed, which she thought would solve her problems, but she still couldn't manage the dog. Blue reacted on a leash, dragged Michelle around, wouldn't come back when called, had separation anxiety, chased her cats, chewed up the couch, and wouldn't eat her food. Blue was extremely frustrated and on several occasions came back at Michelle, acting as if she was going to bite her. The dog didn't bite, but she would grab Michelle's arm.

We met downtown. As we talked, she was constantly touching Blue. She told me she would walk the dog before work, during her lunch break and after work. She had friends who had dogs, so she would meet up with them to let Blue play. As we discussed her life with Blue, I noticed the dog never paid any attention to Michelle. All Blue cared about was everything else going on around her. The dog was really thin and couldn't keep weight on. Michelle had a stressful job, so all the issues with Blue weren't helping. Sometimes she worked long hours and wasn't able to get Blue out for exercise, and so the problems just got worse.

Although Michelle's heart was in the right place, unless she was willing to do a lot of work, Blue was not the best dog for her. Blue came from a place where she had been allowed to roam all day every day. We may not think that is the best thing for the dog, but I'll bet the dog would disagree. Blue once lived on mice or whatever she could find for food, and she never wore a collar or a leash. I'm sure this dog had friends to run and play with, and I'll bet Blue never spent any time indoors. Blue was never exposed to stress or having someone talk to her constantly. She was never taught anything other than survival.

Now, we can own dogs like this, but we need to understand the dog, where it came from and how to adjust this dog from that lifestyle to our lifestyle.

Although Michelle was getting Blue lots of exercise and lots of social time, she was not meeting the dog's mental or nutritional needs. We started by doing basic obedience training, teaching Blue to walk on a leash. Michelle took up running so Blue would be more interested in her movement and we added whole fresh food to the dog's diet. She had a huge fenced backyard. Within the fenced area was a garage. Although not heated, she could leave the door partially open and lay out some straw bales for the dog to settle in for warmth.

This dog was not coping with her stress and living with no mental challenge, and her nutrition was not fueling her body or mind. Blue had very little outdoor time and had lost the ability to roam at random. This new life was stressful for Blue. Michelle was constantly touching her and talking to her, which only added to the dog's stress.

I ask Michelle to quit talking to the dog and only to touch the dog when she was not stressed, and the dog was relaxed. She saw immediate results within 24 hours.

Through time, mental stimulation and a change in nutrition, the dog became a great family pet. She joined dog sports to help with the mental stimulation, their bonding and to continue the social aspect, which was good for both her and the dog.

Famous words I hear almost on a daily basis are, "My dog has a big backyard." How would you like to be in one place day after day after day…? Dogs are curious explorers, rely on their noses and like new adventures. And then we leave them in the same backyard for their entire lives. We never let them out the front door and then wonder why they bolt. My dogs wait in anticipation in the house for me because they are always curious as to what our next adventure is going to be. My dogs relax inside the house because they know there will always be another adventure. It still amazes me how when I take the dogs to a place they have never been. Their noses are so busy exploring this new place!

The Bored Boxer

A couple that owned a boxer called me for lessons. They had always been dog owners, did basic obedience and made sure the dog had friends to play with. The dog was capable of doing all the commands but every time the front door opened, the dog bolted. He had never left the home or yard. The owners had a dog door so he could run from inside to outside whenever he wanted, yet he seemed stressed and had a difficult time settling down.

It was immediately clear to me the boxer had a bond with the male owner. We changed the dog's nutrition and I convinced the owners to start taking the dog out of town and letting him run in an open field or by a canal where he could swim. I wanted the owner to choose different locations and go for walks off-leash with their dog. I ask them to enjoy watching the boxer while walking and to not talk to him too much.

I came back a week later and they had a new dog. The boxer needed to move and explore. The backyard doesn't work! These owners had done many things right but were afraid to let their dog be a dog and roam. They were afraid the boxer would run off and never come back. However, I was not afraid. I could see the bond the dog and owner had. The first few times they went out, I encouraged them to have a friend join them for the walk with another dog that had good recall. I wanted them to only talk to their dog when they were calling the dog back. Reward with touch. "Good dog." Release and say, "Go play." If the dog didn't come on command, just ignore it. The owners enjoyed watching their dog explore so it soon became a regular part of their lives.

The couple was having some marriage issues, as well, so the dog was involved in the stress and needed the off-leash time to release the stress he was absorbing from the owners. In the end, the couple split up, but the man reported that he and the dog were doing very well. Out of all the dogs he had ever owned, he had never had a bond with a dog like he did with this one. He was grateful to learn there was more to dog ownership than just obedience training.

Mona and Jake

Complete chaos has been my response in leaving many homes over the years. Upon arrival, the dog will be jumping all over me, Mom will be crying because she now has more stress in her life, the kids won't like the pup anymore because he is using them as their favourite chew toy, all the shoes are chewed up, the dog won't quit barking and he will be peeing and pooping in the house. Most people just don't understand that all the behaviours your dog is doing are choices he is making. You need to teach them to make good choices, which results in good behaviour. If you don't mentally challenge your dogs, you will always have chaos.

A young mother with a husband and two children called when their new pup arrived. She was overwhelmed with having a new puppy and babies in the home. Upon arrival, everything I mentioned above was happening. We fitted Jake with a collar and attached the pup to Mom. This way she was able to control him while doing things with the children. Jake was not able to chew on the children, and if he acted incorrectly, she could respond and teach him without chasing after him.

Although Jake was young, he had already learned he would get attention every time he jumped on someone, chewed on the kids, peed on the floor or played with shoes. I taught Mom how to keep Jake attached to her and how to give the command *SIT*. When the leash was dragging, she could grab it and not the dog. The husband agreed to walk Jake every night after he got home from work. I worked with Mom for six weeks, teaching Jake all the basic commands, and her husband continued to walk him. She had a friend with a pup, so they swapped dog daycare a couple of times a week, so the social needs of both of the dogs were met, and Mom started feeding Jake a species-appropriate diet.

By the end of the six weeks, when I would arrive, Jake would be lying on its bed and Mom was much happier. Basic obedience is critical for mental stimulation for the dog and is a great way for you to learn how to handle a leash to control the dog. Lack of control is chaos!

Food Matters!

You may not think food is important, but I want you to consider what nutrition does for our health. Whole, living, raw and fresh food is so important to our physical and mental health.

A young mom living out on a farm called me to help with her new pup. She thought something was wrong with him. She had owned several dogs in the past, but this dog seemed to struggle with learning and understanding the very basic commands. She didn't want the pup jumping on the kids or her mom. The dog wouldn't stay out of the kibble or any garbage lying around. For two weeks, we worked on basic obedience exercises, but I was as frustrated as the owner because we were not gaining any ground. Every time I arrived to work with her, the dog wanted to jump all over me.

She had inquired the week before about raw food for dogs. I brought out a case of food for her to try. We worked on her body language and a few more basic commands and then discussed the raw food. The following week, she cancelled class because the dog had hurt its toe. Two weeks later, we met, and the dog was totally different. He did not jump on me. He was calm and eager to please and he complied with all the commands.

Because the owner was young and healthy and understood how important nutrition is to our overall wellbeing, she wanted to try the raw food for her dogs. She totally believed we are what we eat, so the same should be true for our dogs. I, too, am a believer of whole, living, fresh or raw foods. I have seen the difference in mental and physical benefits for many dogs when they switch to a species-appropriate diet. I believe processed food is difficult for a dog to digest and it can make them uncomfortable. Dogs need to drink a ton of water to push out the food (poop). Raw fed dogs don't drink as much, as the food can process through their system within a half an hour. Their bodies absorb the nutrition, so they don't poop much, the small bones keep their teeth clean and their breath is fresh. If your dog is satisfied nutritionally, this helps to create that calm, relaxed dog you desire.

Conclusion

Not all dogs are the same. Many factors affect how a dog adjusts to our world. When a dog is naughty, it is our responsibility to find out what is happening with him. Most often it is related to a lack of something.

What Works: consistency, using strong body language, moving with speed and purpose, touching your dog only for a job well done or in play, letting your dog off-leash at times, finding some friends for your dog and feeding a quality species-appropriate diet. Over time, you will create the well-mannered companion you want.

Action Plan
1) To have a calm dog, your environment must be calm.
2) Don't leave food lying around. Feed your dog twice a day after you have eaten. This is most important during the training stage. Puppies should be fed three times daily until they are a year old.
3) Dogs need at least 45 minutes of exercise twice daily. Some of this time should be off-leash with dog friends and some should be on-leash working on leash skills.
4) Train basics such as *SIT, STAY, DOWN* and *COME*. These commands teach you how to handle a leash and provide the dog with great mental stimulation.
5) Dogs need a species-appropriate diet, so provide them with the nutrition they need to be healthy both mentally and physically.
6) Touch your dog only when it is doing the behaviour you want. Don't reinforce bad behavior through touch.
7) Exposure to people is especially important during the pup's 8-16 weeks. If you have a young puppy, make sure he meets as many people and dogs as possible. (Meet and greet with people and dogs you know are healthy and in spaces that are clean and free from common disease — parvo, for example). Use your backyard or a friend's backyard. Take your pup to the office where you work, if allowed, to meet your coworkers.

8) Because they live through their noses, to keep things interesting for your dog after their vaccines have been completed, choose several places to walk your dog. Find new and exciting paths daily for your dog's adventure!
9) If you work full time, you may want to consider a dog daycare two days a week to help stimulate your dog.
10) If you are stressed while training, your dog will also be stressed. Have fun!

Measure of Success:

Is your dog getting daily off-leash time? How many human and dog friends does your dog have? Are you touching the dog only when he does the behaviour you want?

CHAPTER 3

Becoming the Expert

In order for you to be the expert, you must understand dog behaviour, be consistent, meet your dog's needs, have expectations, create rules, talk to a dog when necessary but not constantly, understand hierarchy, be a leader, understand how to handle a leash, understand that obedience training gives your dog work to do, understand that your voice or high-pitched noises may upset the dog, comprehend how important touch and movement are to the dog and moving with speed and purpose creates interest for your dog, understand pressure and release, clear up your communication with your dog, know your dog needs friends, dogs need a species-appropriate diet, dogs learn from older dogs and dogs make lots of noise when they are having fun!

Every dog is different. Over time you will begin to understand your dog. Breeds, personalities, the owner's lifestyles, and food each play a role in how a dog develops and grows.

First of all, keeping four paws on the floor is so important. You must always pick up your dog if the dog is in danger, but for no other reason. When the dog is on the ground they get to explore the world. If you pick up your dog, they are missing out on all the smells, which is a huge part of the dog's world. When your dog is required to be on the ground, they learn how to deal with life. When we protect our children too much, it is not always for the best. The same goes for your dog. Picking up your dog takes away from his learning opportunities - how to deal with people, other dogs, cars, strange noises, or trains, for example. When we curl up the dog around us, especially if we are nervous, we create an anxious dog. How many times have you seen a dog that is growling or snapping when the owner is holding him? Carrying a dog does not build his confidence. Obedience training, off-leash time with friends, good nutrition, and four paws on the floor creates a confident dog.

Consistency will be the big winner over time. When you ask a dog to *SIT* or lie *DOWN* as you open the door, but then the next day you are too busy and don't request the same obedience out of your dog, you can't question why the training exercises aren't working. Dogs are either instinctual learners or repetitive learners. Whatever type of learner your dog may be, the minimum your dog must do a command such as *SIT* is at least 200 times, and for some breeds up to a 1000 times, before the dog actually knows with 100% certainty the command you are asking. If you don't believe me, track asking your dog to *SIT* 200 times. Then test your dog. Without the dog seeing you, ask the dog to *SIT*. If the dog sits, they know the command. If they don't sit, you still have work to do. In the beginning, using your body to help the dog understand what you're asking helps a great deal, but then to make each exercise more difficult, you have to change your body position, get out of their sight or turn your back on the dog and then see if the dog will still do the exercise. Or when your dog goes to the front door and sits to wait for the leash to be attached, you know the dog understands what behaviour you want from them.

Hierarchy is how a dog lives. You are either below or above the dog, never equal. When your dog clearly understands its position within your family, he will be more willing to defer to you, please you and be a part of your pack.

A martingale collar creates pressure or release when the handler understands how to use a leash properly. The collar and leash will clear up any confusion your dog may be experiencing. Give pressure when the dog is in the wrong position and release when they do as you ask. Your dog will struggle in the beginning but be consistent by applying pressure on the collar with the leash, and the dog will sit. He'll quickly understand what you are asking and will do the exercise with no words necessary to achieve the command. If your dog is struggling, look at your body language. Are you standing tall with confidence, shoulders back, feet apart?

Pampered Pooch

Over the years, I have had several clients who refuse to keep the dog's paws on the floor. We don't seem to care when a five-pound dog bites us, but we care when the dog weighs 100 pounds. There is no difference, just what we think is okay to tolerate. Four paws on the floor creates confidence in any size dog.

A coworker asked if she could bring her ten-pound dog to class one evening. She was concerned about the young dog's behaviour. He only went outdoors to take care of business and she carried him everywhere (even when she walked her older dog). The dog had started to pee and poop in the house. If you stepped close to my coworker, the dog would growl and snap. He got no off-leash time and had no friends. She wondered how the dog would do with a group of dogs. I told her she could come but that the dog had to stay on the ground. We fitted the dog with a quality collar and leash, and she showed up that evening.

When they arrived, I told everyone to ignore the dog. I knew he would scream trying to manipulate the owner into picking him up. The owner was good and left the dog on the ground. I told her to walk around the dogs with the leash loose, close enough to smell but not touch. All the other clients were asked to put their dog in a *SIT*. After she moved around with the dog for a bit, he did a big old shake, which meant he was relieving his stress, so we began class. That night we had great fun with the dogs. The class was fast paced, going over obstacles, lots of *SITS* and *STAYS*, climbing stairs, over tables, climbing big rocks and working on the command *DOWN*.

At the end of the class, I let the dog engage in a meeting with all the clients in class. I ask everyone to go over and pet the dog. There was no growling or snapping. One class with the dog being allowed to be a dog.

Can you imagine what six or eight weeks of training would do for this dog? The owner could not believe the difference in her dog. She signed up for the remainder of this training session. What a lovely dog she owned once the spoiling was gone. Prior to class, this dog was under a year old and was headed in the wrong direction. The next time I saw her out walking with her dogs, both dogs had four paws on the ground!

Daily Practice

When I teach group classes, the first two weeks are fantastic. All the clients follow the instructions. Connected with the dog for two weeks, they limit the amount of talking to the dog, four paws on the floor, the owners move with speed and purpose, owners only touch the dog when they are calm or do the exercise right and they make the dog *SIT* for everything. But then comes Week Three. No homework has been done. The dogs are not paying attention and we need to go back to the Week One lesson. Consistency ends, the owner is tired of having expectations, the dog starts to readjust the hierarchy position and we go back to all the bad behaviour.

Teaching a dog is not about one or two classes a week for an hour and then go home and do nothing. Teaching a dog is about using every day to have expectations for your dog, giving them something constructive to do. For example, you go to the front door. Your dog must *SIT*. Attach the leash, walk out the front door and the dog comes with you. While you are making supper, the dog must lay in his bed. When you see the dog looking at you, clap your hands, open your arms and get your dog to come to you. Using a leash, connect your dog to you as you are cooking supper, doing laundry, watching TV, taking the baby for a walk in the stroller or going for a run. When a dog is connected to you, they can't get into trouble.

Spending extra time in your day training your dog is not necessary but setting your dog up for success and uses everyday opportunities to teach as necessary. The more consistent you are with your expectations, the quicker the dog will not challenge the hierarchy position in the family. When you do notice the dog challenging his position, just go back to the basics to get the dog back on track.

A young couple requested my help with their pup. Mom was stressed, dad worked outside the home and they had three children, one still not in school. They got a puppy that had extremely high energy. Week after week, I would go to their home and nothing had changed. The dog had no rules, they didn't apply any of my suggestions I'd made, they had 101 excuses why they couldn't apply the exercises and the dog had a full run of the house and knew it.

The kids were constantly crying and yelling because the pup was chasing them, and the parents laughed because they thought it was funny. Each week, they newly committed to applying the exercises I'd given them, putting the dog in a crate a couple times a day to calm him down and agreeing to give the dog some off-leash time to burn off excess energy. Yet every week, nothing had changed. Nobody wanted to be around this dog. Family and friends didn't want to visit and be around a dog with no manners.

Only you can make the decision to commit to training and be consistent with your dog. I can help you understand dog behaviour, but you need to teach your pup and then be consistent.

Your dog training efforts will not be as successful if you aren't willing to be consistent and increase expectations as the dog learns and grows.

Who's the Boss?

Time and time again, I see dogs in a class, in people's homes or walking down the street, and the dog is controlling everything. It gets so bad that the owners refuse to take their dogs out on walks or to let them off-leash. Owners quit coming to obedience class and leave the dog out in the backyard to bark, dig or chase the neighbour's dog along the fence line.

I see daily posts on social media of people wanting to rehome their dog because the dog chases cats, the dog shouldn't be around children or other dogs or the dog needs a farm where it will have more room to roam. These are all actions of a dog that is making its own decisions. Because the owners are not teaching yet they don't like the decisions the dog is making, the owners want to rehome him instead. Don't get me wrong, there may be valid reasons to rehome a dog, but from my experience, most dogs respond in a fantastic way when all of their needs are met. Rehoming may not be necessary.

Mary was a farm wife who rescued a mix breed for some protection out on the farm. She called for help when no one could enter their yard unless the dog was locked up in his outdoor kennel or inside the house. This was a problem, because the farm had hired hands to help so people were coming and going all the time. They were tired of having the dog kenneled all the time. They really wanted the dog to be able to wander with the helpers as they worked and spend time with her when she was outdoors. We talked on the phone for a while. I asked her to put a martingale collar on the dog, attach a six-foot leash and put a muzzle on him. When I arrived, she was to do as she had always done when anyone pulled into the yard.

As soon as I entered the yard, the dog lunged at the end of the leash. She was pulling back, making him *SIT* and wrapping the leash around her hand. When the dog was sitting, it was baring teeth at me. She was petting the dog and telling him everything was going to be okay. I asked them to kennel the dog so we could chat. I explained to them how everything they'd done was reinforcing the dog's behaviour — the pulling back, wrapping the leash, touching the dog when it was stressed and worse of all, performing these behaviors when she was extremely stressed. All of this confirmed what the dog believed to be true, that every person who entered the yard was a threat!

I ask her son to go get the dog. Even if the dog hit the end of the leash, he was to keep walking and turn the opposite direction. Whatever direction the dog wanted to go he was to go the opposite. At no time could there be pressure on the leash. The son had to continue to move, walking around the yard. I instructed her son to move quickly, keeping the dog's attention on him. As he moved around, I watched the tension in the dog waver. Eventually, we were all walking together.

The hired men were working outside the shop. I told the son to walk closer to the men. Every time the dog's head moved slightly toward the men, he was to pick up speed, snap the leash a little and get the dog's attention back on him. The more the dog responded and shook off the stress, the closer we got to the men.

Finally we were all standing in a group talking. The dog relaxed and laid down. I told her son to reward the dog with touch because he was relaxed in a place that had given him huge discomfort only a short while before. I instructed everyone not to look at the dog or touch him unless the dog came over to them. They were to let the dog sniff, but still ignore the dog until he nudged them for attention. At that point, I still didn't want anyone to make eye contact — just to touch the dog.

Over the next six weeks, I worked with Mary to build both her confidence and the dog's. She learned the importance of how her emotions were affecting the dog, how what she was doing with touch and wrapping the leash confirmed to the dog there was a problem and that she could clear up the communication between her and the dog to get better results. We covered all the basic obedience commands to give the dog some mental stimulation and discussed nutrition.

Mary's dog was scared, lacking confidence, had no daily structure and was spending too much time in the kennel because she felt she couldn't trust him. I told her to leave the muzzle on until she was confident the dog wasn't going to bite her. Mary needed to relax and learn to trust the dog, and if the muzzle gave her confidence, she was to leave it on. The dog was actually all talk and no bite, but Mary was nervous, and this was creating insecurity in him.

Leader does not mean *Alpha*. It means building a relationship with your dog, so he looks to you for guidance. Dogs want to be led. They want to make you happy and they want to do as you ask. That is what dogs do! Teach your dog what you want him to do and he will comply. If you don't take the time to teach him, he will be left confused, which leads to a lack of confidence.

Dog Communication Secrets

If you completely understand how to use a martingale collar and a leash, you will clear up any and all of your communication problems with your dog. This is truly the only way you can communicate with a dog. The sole purpose of a martingale collar is pressure and release. When the dog is in the wrong position, the collar becomes tight, and when he is doing as you ask, the collar releases the pressure. I have not seen a dog yet that doesn't respond to this type of learning. Your dog will quickly think through and understand what you're asking when the pressure of the collar is applied and then immediate released when he does what he has been asked to do. For example, when you draw up on the leash (pressure), the dog's bum hits the ground (release). Within a short period of time, the dog will sit as soon as you start to draw up on the leash (pressure). Pressure and release, along with strong solid body language, gives your dog clear communication.

Recently, an associate of mine got a young pup. They informed me the dog did not want to wear a collar and thrashed on the leash. We fitted the pup with a martingale collar, and I requested that for the first week to just let the pup drag a small, light leash around the house when they were at home with the dog. When we met the next time, I showed them how to draw up on the leash to get the dog to *SIT*. We talked about the importance of the pup wearing a collar and how the pressure and release worked. I handled the leash and managed the first several *SITS*. The owners could not believe how easily the dog would sit. They had tried several methods and the dog would not consistently *Sit*. Before I left that day, we had the dog in a *SIT and STAY*. The owner dropped the leash and was walking around the room with the dog staying in a *SIT* until he was released.

Along with teaching the owners how important their body language was to the dog and how consistency is important to the dog's learning ability, we had a successful training day. Later that evening, they messaged me to say they could not believe the difference in their dog. Even the children came home from school and wondered why the dog was so calm. When the owners cleared up the communication, used proper body language, and had expectations, the pup immediately jumped on board with the training.

Conclusion

It can be simple to have a well-mannered dog. Let your dog have all four paws on the floor at all times. Be consistent! Make sure your dog understands his place in your family. Communicate clearly using the leash and the martingale collar. It is important for your dog to have rules. Ask only once and then expect your dog to follow the command you gave. Dogs are simple creatures. We make it complicated and overthink everything we do with our dogs. Teach your dog to make good choices so you can trust him!

Action Plan:

1) The dog must have all four paws on the floor at all times.
2) Decide what the family rules are for the dog and then be consistent in asking him to follow your rules. List five rules.
3) Buy a calendar and put a mark on the calendar for each day that you ask the dog to *SIT, STAY, DOWN* and *COME*. This needs to be done consistently for six weeks, asking the dog to perform the commands at least ten times per day. Some dogs will require more.
4) What is your position from the dog's point of view? Are you above, below or equal? You need to be above. Dogs view everything, human or canine, in order of hierarchy. Your dog needs to know where it belongs in your family pack.

5) Pressure on the martingale collar is asking the dog to do the command. Release is the reward for doing the command. The release needs to be immediate!

SIT: Draw up on the leash (pressure) in a bicep curl. When the dog's bum hits the ground, immediately release. As soon as the dog is moving his bum to the ground, with very little pressure on the leash, apply the command word *SIT*.

Example of Five Rules:
1) Four paws on the floor at all times.
2) Dog sleeps in a crate.
3) No jumping!
4) Dog plays outdoors.
5) Dog eats last. Feed your family first.

Measure of Success:
   Do you drag the leash so you can teach the dog when it is making the wrong choice? Does the dog have four paws on the floor at all times? Is everyone in the house consistent with the rules? Does your dog *SIT* as soon as you apply a little bit of pressure on the leash?

CHAPTER 4

It's Not What You "Think"

As humans, we assume dogs think, react, love, play, socialize, eat, and enjoy life exactly like we do. However, this is not always true. For a large part, dogs think counterintuitively to how we think. Let's go through some of these things so I can help you understand what I mean.

Dogs do not think like we do. They have no ability to reason. Instead, they react to everything that happens around them. Dogs mimic what you do. You smile and your dog smiles. You act mad and your dog will cower away. If your tone of voice goes deep with, "Did you do that?" your dog will look shamed. If you keep your body soft and happy, your dog will approach you. If you're mad and are stomping around, your dog will stay away.

Dogs don't reason. You ask, and they'll decide to comply or ignore you based on your energy (are you happy), body language and how willing they are to obey (mental stimulation or obedience training). In no way will a dog approach a person who is yelling, screaming, or chasing them with their arms flinging around in the air, or that person who is calling the dog, "Buddy, Buddy, Buddy. BUddy!! BUDdy!!! BUDDy!!!! BUDDY!!!!! Goddamn it, BUDDY." Nope. Not going to happen. The dog will stay away.

Clair and Kip

One of my favourite dogs in the world is Kip. He is an 80lb German Shepherd and has a great owner. We became friends when Kip's owners hired me to work with them. We did both private and group training and off-leash walks. They invested the time and energy required to train a dog, changed his food to a species-appropriate diet, and to this day, the owners say out of all the German shepherds she has owned, Kip is that great dog we all hope for. Her bond with this dog is incredible. One day we went for an off-leash walk. As we got back to the car, we opened the back end of our SUV and Kip took off. We assumed he felt he hadn't gotten enough time outdoors. We continued to walk around and ignore him, but he knew better and wouldn't come close to us at all. The owner couldn't believe it! As time went on, the owner was getting madder and madder, even though she was still using a soft tone. Kip knew!

I finally asked her to leave. I told her I would call when I had him. She got in her car, Kip watched her leave, and then he went about his business. I went and sat on a bench. I totally ignored him. No talking, no eye contact, no stress. I took five deep breaths because I wanted any negative energy to leave my body. I hadn't even sat there for five minutes before Kip came up and nudged me in the arm. I loaded Kip up and called Clair. She hadn't even arrived at home yet. The moral of the story is, if you are stressed, your dog knows it and they'll want nothing to do with you.

I LOVE YOU SO MUCH!

Of course we love our dogs! Love to most people is cuddling on the couch, letting the dog sleep in our beds, carrying the dog everywhere, hugging, feeding the dog tons of treats with no nutritional value and talking to the dog constantly. There is nothing wrong with most of this, except the bad treats and talking constantly, but I'll bet your dog loves long walks, playing with their puppy friends, doing sports, off-leash time, and leashed walks. Movement and touch is everything to a dog, so when we move with our dogs, that is how we show our love for them. When we reward them with touch, the dog is pleased they have done what we expected. Then, after a busy, active day of training, walking and friends we can cuddle on the couch. All I ask, is that you do what the dog loves first, and then do what we think is love afterward. I have seen many monsters created by only loving the dog from our view and not both views. It's mutual respect which gets the best results.

Every day I hear, "I love my dog so much!" I do too, but love doesn't create a well-mannered dog. Love without discipline may create a monster that you or anybody else don't want to be around.

Jill and Frank

Years ago an elderly couple contacted me about their little dog. This dog maybe weighed 15lbs, but it was a monster! The dog would drag Jill down streets, he growled and barked at everyone, he was peeing and pooping in the house and had most recently started to pee and poop in her husband's bed.

Her husband spent most of his day in bed due to health reasons. The dog would lie on top of him. He would constantly feed the dog treats and the dog received physical touch all day. The dog was getting older, as well, and had never had any other interactions with people or dogs, other than when she tried to take the dog for a walk.

Recently, the dog had dragged her down the sidewalk, she fell and was bruised all over. When she went into the bedroom to help care for her husband, the dog would growl and lunge at her. Plus, as I stated earlier, the dog was now peeing and pooping in her husband's bed. This couple was devastated by the dog's behaviour and couldn't understand what had gone wrong. They loved this dog! Their reasoning was as long as they loved the dog, he would never do anything to them.

Within two weeks of me starting to work with them to change the dog's behaviour the dog bit her husband. One of the daughters came over to visit. When she walked into the bedroom, the dog growled and lunged as she got closer to her dad. The family didn't believe the dog would ever bite because they "loved" the dog, and yet here we were. The guy who "loved" the dog the most was the guy who ended up getting bit! The whole family was confused and couldn't understand why the dog had bit Dad.

Jill decided to hand the dog over to a rescue that specialized in that breed. After rehabilitation, the dog was placed in a home that provided leadership, rules, expectations and then love.

When we choose love over leadership, rules, expectations, and obedience training the dog gets confused and pays the price for not making good decisions. Love your dog but show your love in ways that are most important for the dog's physical, mental, and social health first, and then get the love you require back.

Freedom versus Responsibility

Most dogs love to play. Like everything in life, if there is not a balance, it can lead to a monster dog. Dogs that spend too much time playing are at risk of injury. When dogs are moving naturally, they will walk, run, dig, play with other dogs, and then move again. Even when dogs are on an off-leash walk, you will rarely see dogs just play. They will play for a minute or two and then roam.

Take your dog somewhere safe and let him go. Watch what he chooses to do. If you keep walking and moving, so will he. If you stand in one spot he will stay close by. I will only go out with a group of people if they agree to walk. Off-leash time is about the dog's movement. It can be a social time for you, as well, but keep moving. When people and dogs quit moving tension may rise. I demonstrate this exercise when I hold a group training session. When you move, dogs play and run. When you stop moving, the dogs circle around the people and tension starts to rise in the dogs. When you're moving, even if the dogs are getting tense, they will smell something, get distracted, shake it off and keep going. I call this freedom and responsibility.

Dogs that get too much freedom do not make good decisions. You as the dog owner need to create a balance of freedom and responsibility. Dogs love to run and play, even though this is important, work on commands until you have an obedient dog.

A group of women ask me to join them one afternoon with their dogs. I decided to go out and visit with them. When I arrived with Reba, they were all just standing in one spot visiting and the dogs were all hovering around their feet almost knocking them over. The ladies all had a coffee and were enjoying their visit. We walked into the park and I released Reba from her leash because I don't like dogs meeting each other with a leash attached. The dogs immediately charged at Reba, who became overwhelmed. The owners of the other dogs were calling and yelling at their dogs to leave Reba alone, but of course, the dogs did not listen to their owners.

Reba took off running. The other dog owners chased after their dogs in their vehicles. However, I sat and waited for Reba to come back, which she did. This is a good example of freedom and responsibility not being in balance. In this group of dogs, there were a couple of dogs that had no structure or rules. Problems may arise when a couple of dogs in a group teach all the other dogs bad behaviours. At some point, a dog or person is going to get hurt. You should never trust giving your dog one way to burn off energy. Off-leash play with no structure is the worst way to burn up a dog's energy.

Go for a walk with your friends and let your dogs go off leash. If you can only go to an off-leash park, walk, don't stand around. Movement is so important for a dog, even when they have friends to play with.

Masters of Human Body Language

Dogs have lived with humans for centuries and have evolved to understand our body language better than any human understands human body language. They are the experts of us. They watch us, react to us, come to us when we are sad, stay away when they know we are mad, and some dogs have shown people when they are sick. Dogs can do amazing things, but I believe it is because they understand us. Now we just need to understand them.

You have the right to believe anything you want, but I challenge you to stop over-talking to your dog, bending over to your dog, watching for your dog, moving for your dog and carrying your dog. Within 24-48 hours, you will see that your body language is truly what your dog relies on to function in our world. When we do all the things I mentioned above, the dog doesn't have to pay attention, so we aren't giving them something to do.

If their job becomes watching us, we create constructive work for the dog to do. We are now setting them up for success and teaching.

Dave, Deb, and Pal

Pal, an Australian shepherd about 12 weeks old, was registered for my spring session. The first night of class I requested the owners to leave their dogs in the vehicle so we could discuss how we were going to start class and give them general guidelines for everyone to follow. When everyone went and got their dogs from their vehicles, I immediately noticed how Pal was reacting. He was nervous, his tail was tucked, he didn't want to engage with any other dogs and was crying and jumping around, trying to hide. The owners constantly gave him attention when he acted scared. They stood in one spot and picked up Pal when they thought he was scared. As class progressed, Pal got worse.

During the first class of a program, we discuss all the important things humans do (act), so everyone understands why dogs do what they do (react). We discuss body language, the importance of the dog having four paws on the floor, how talking too much and touching the dog at the wrong time can affect the dog and how feeding a species-appropriate diet is a huge asset to the dog's physical and mental health. We then connect the dogs to us for the remainder of the class. Homework for the first week is connecting the dog to you for two hours daily.

The next class came along. Again, we met at an outdoor location. When Pal got out of the vehicle, it was shocking to say the least. He had gone from a scared, nervous dog to a confident dog in four days. What a change. I asked them what they had done. These owners had followed all the rules. They'd done all the homework and in just four days we had a happy, fun-loving pup! He was ready to work, engaged the other dogs and then played after class with the other pups.

People do many things to try and help their pup when they think they are nervous or scared, but in fact it is because of our body language and our concern that we are telling the pup there is in fact something to be nervous and scared about. Dave and Deb did the right thing for Pal and they were on their way to a confident, happy, healthy pup that will work for them and make good decisions.

Conclusion

I hope you can see now how the actions we take that may make us feel good or we think are helping the dog are in fact creating behaviours in dogs that over time develop into problems for the owners but mostly affect the dogs. The dog will be the one that suffers the consequences because he lacks confidence and does not make good decisions. This creates chaos in the home. Be calm, play with your dog, teach first then give the dog freedom. Love happens with a balance of freedom and responsibility. Your dog understands your body language better than you understand theirs.

Take the time to learn about dogs and what works for them instead of doing what is right for you or what makes sense from your perspective. You have invited dogs into your home, so it is your responsibility to provide a healthy, balanced lifestyle for them.

Action Plan:

1) Be calm!
2) Check your body language: stand tall, feet shoulder width apart, shoulders back.
3) Continue to ask the dog to follow your rules.
4) Incorporate *SIT* and *STAY* into your daily routine.

SIT/STAY — Draw up on the leash, asking the dog to *SIT*. Pivot in front of the dog, hand out in front of you, asking the dog to *STAY*. No eye contact, strong body language. After 30 seconds, pivot back to a heel position and with the leg closest to the dog release the dog just by moving your foot and commanding, "*All Done.*"

Measure of Success:

Can your dog SIT and *STAY* for 10 minutes?

CHAPTER 5

The Past is Irrelevant

Dogs are so amazing! I got Reba when she was 16 months old. I believe in training my dog, so I applied all my ideas for eight weeks. I attached her to me for two hours a day, she got to run off-leash daily, I put her in with a good group of dogs so she could meet new friends, took her to all of my training lessons and fed her a species-appropriate diet. I would sit on the floor in the evening to play with her. I rarely talked to her and I only touched her when she did exactly what I wanted. I would make her think through the process of what I wanted so she was mentally stimulated. When I brought her home, I didn't care what had happened in her past. I just wanted to build her confidence so I could rely on her when I was working with clients. My old guy Brady had retired, and I was missing having a partner in class.

Reba

Everyone who came to our home would make comments such as, "Oh, she is scared," or, "Why is she so timid?" or, "What's wrong with her? Was she abused?"

I got Reba from a friend and associate. I know for a fact that she was NOT abused. I tell you this because these are common statements I hear from clients who have rescued a dog and they behave in a manner that people assume is "timid." Human nature makes us respond by pitying dog. People assume he had a bad life and that is why he was in a shelter. We assume the previous owners didn't treat the dog right, or he got taken away from the home because they were bad owners. Then the dog cowers when we stare at it or try to get near and touch him. I'm not saying there are terrible stories out there about dogs and abuse. I will never understand how anyone can hurt a dog or abuse a helpless animal.

But f in my experience, most dogs in a shelter are there because the owners had to move, the owners have health issues, or they bought a dog that was not a good fit for their family. If you fall in love with that dog at a shelter, take the dog home and treat it just as if you were bringing home a puppy from a breeder. Set up a training plan, get the dog out for some exercise, find your new family member some friends and continue on with your life, including structured rules and expectations for your dog. That is what a dog understands. He will adjust to your life in a very short period of time. I tell all my clients to allow the dog two weeks to adjust once you take him home and then start with formal training, whether he is a puppy from a breeder or a dog from a shelter. You are going to have this dog for the next 10-15 years, so set up a routine and teach your dog so he will become the best companion for you and your family.

I want you to consider something I said earlier — dogs only react! When you bring the dog home, he is only reacting to what we are doing.

Now let's talk about Reba again. People would come into our home, rush up to her, make eye contact, bend over her, try to pick her up and move quickly, which would scare her. Not one person ever considered leaving her alone to let her come to them when she was ready. Before you have a bond with a dog, eye contact is a threat! Reba the border collie responds to anything that moves fast. Bending over a dog makes any dog uncomfortable. Although people like picking up dogs, dogs really prefer four paws on the floor.

Like everyone else, I could have assumed Reba was scared or abused. I could have come to my own conclusions about her past life, not exposed her to anything and quit walking her or socializing her with other dogs. My question is, though, how would that have helped Reba? That's not the way to achieve a healthy, balanced dog. So we got busy and set up a routine, changed her diet, started training and found some friends. Now, at age three, she totally amazes me. I could bore you with her incredible stories.

The first time we went back to see her original owner she was so excited. As soon as I got close to the property where she was born, she hopped up with excitement and couldn't wait to see Chris and all the other dogs she had spent time with. Training Reba created an incredible bond between us and every day I laugh and learn from her.

To "rescue" a dog is a great way to become a dog owner, but please don't feel sorry for the dog. Understand that you are providing the dog with a great life. Start a training program , give your dog some off-leash time, leashed walks, good nutrition, and friends. Dogs really don't require a lot to make them happy. Don't look back. Move forward!

Rescue

A young couple in our community rescued a dog that was found roaming in Northern Alberta. They were an active couple and had just started their family. They decide to enroll in one of my programs. This couple had no experience as dog owners. They were willing to learn and wholeheartedly engage and apply the lessons to the best of their ability just so they could have the best family companion before their son arrived. Each week they would come back to class and show me how well their dog was learning the lessons.

They continued to ask good questions, be creative while adding challenges for their dog, and even started trusting the dog to do off-leash adventures! Dad was a runner, so he and the dog would go for a run in the morning, while Mom worked on leash skills so she would be able to walk the baby and the dog all at the same time. During class, they would take turns working with the dog. They never questioned what I asked them to do. They understood that if I was asking, they would learn something from the process.

To date, this is one of the dogs that brings me the most pride. You may never have owned a dog and yet you can still rescue one. If you are willing to put some time and energy into your dog, you will create a great family companion.

They have now moved away, but on occasion they send me pictures of their family, which is much larger now, and the dog is always included.

Verna, Nick, and Leo

One of my first clients years ago was a black Lab. Leo was six years old and had been adopted from the local shelter. He was the only dog not barking when Nick entered the shelter. Nick, nine years old at the time, was immediately smitten. They took Leo home for a day to meet Grandpa, who was living with them at that time. They fell in love and promptly brought Leo home.

They began training immediately and joined up with some agility, as well. Leo and Nick were having fun! The benefits of training were seen in quite a short time, even though Leo was six. At Leo's last home he was digging out of the backyard and bolting every chance he got.

Behaviour like this is hard to change and requires consistency and patience. Although very frustrating at times for Verna and Nick, they continued to work with Leo. Leo had full-time companionship with Grandpa living in the home, as well as three cats. Now, at 14.5 years of age, Leo is happy, healthy, and living the best life ever!

Conclusion

You never know what you are in for when you rescue a dog from a shelter, a friend, or an associate. But what I do know for sure is if you treat that dog as if he is the newest member of the pack and don't feel sorry for him, you can end up with an amazing companion for your family. Apply structure, rules, and expectations. You will have some work to do, but it will definitely be worth the effort.

Action Plan:

1) Don't feel sorry for the dog. You are now providing him with a loving home. Your focus needs to be on the future, not the past.
2) No excuses! Just start training.
3) Apply structure, rules, and expectations.
4) Be aware of your body language.
5) Set your dog up for success through training.
6) Work up to a 30-minute *SIT/STAY*.

Measure of Success:

Is the dog calm? Does the dog respect your rules and expectations? Can you see when you change your body language how the dog responds?

CHAPTER 6

Who Makes the Rules?

When I enter a home, it is always apparent when the dog is making all the rules and the owners are living by those rules. For the most, part the owners often aren't even aware until I point out what the dog is doing. He is charging at me as I enter, and he has no rules. Owners will say the dog is just protecting its home. The dog is blocking me or jumping all over me, controlling my movement. The owner will say the dog is just excited to see me and loves people so much. The dog is barking, growling and running toward me and then hiding with its tail tucked. He is manipulating the owner. The owner will say the dog is nervous around people, or I am scaring her dog and the dog has never behaved that way before. The dog backs up or hides with no confidence. The owner will laugh and think it's funny. The dog grabs my arm, controlling my movement. The owner will let the dog do it because they are afraid to correct the dog. Whatever behaviour your dog has, it has purpose and meaning to the dog. Dogs are masters at manipulation because they know and understand our body language so well. Your dog is reacting! Either through reward or touch, the dog is making up the rules in the house and the dog cannot be trusted.

Tilley the Terror!

A young couple with three small boys at home called me to come out to their home in a small community close to where I live. The husband wasn't home, but I met with the wife. When I arrived, the dog charged at me, hitting the front door before I even entered. To tell you the honest truth, I was nervous. I ask the wife, Shelly, to leash the dog and remove her from the front door. She did and then I entered the home. I kept my body soft so as to not challenge the dog. When I got into the home, any time I moved, the dog would react and come at me. Shelly was terrified Tilley might hurt me. She already had her hands full with her three small children and didn't have time to spend with the dog.

Her husband wanted a dog in the home because he worked away and thought protection for Shelley and the boys would be good. I eventually told her to drop the leash. The dog stared at me, but we continued to talk and eventually Tilley went and curled up on the couch. I ask Shelly, "What will happen if you try to pull the dog off the couch?" She honestly had no idea because she had always just let the dog do whatever she wanted.

Because the leash was dragging, I asked her to go grab it and then pull Tilley off. She did and the dog growled and snapped at her. She then told me that recently, Tilley had growled and snapped at her boys when they walked by the dog's kennel. She admitted she was terrified of the dog and started to cry.

Her husband was not willing to give Tilley up because he felt better with the dog in the home. What he didn't understand was the dog was most likely eventually going to bite one of his family members. Shelley then proceeded to tell me the dog had once grabbed a neighbor kid by the back of the leg when the boys were outside playing. The boy went home crying and the other parents had called the police.

This led to the dog being tied up outside. Now Tilley got no exercise, Shelley was terrified, and the dog was tied up when it was outside or in the kennel in the house. Yet if Tilley was outside of the kennel, the dog was allowed to do whatever she wanted because she was scared.

This is a prime example of a dog making all the decisions. When a dog makes all the decisions, they are normally not the best decisions, which can then result in bad behaviour. Tilley was set up for failure and never had a chance. Because none of the dog's needs were met, Tilley decided she was going to protect her space. Dogs that protect their families can change their boundaries daily and this may become dangerous.

We worked on a few things and I guided Shelley on how she could handle some of these situations. We were to meet the following week. They called me before our next session. Tilley had broken loose in the backyard, jumped the fence and bit another neighbourhood kid again. The bite was serious. They handed the dog over to a rescue that agreed to work with Tilley and placed her in a new home.

Jake the Jumper

Jake will be this generic dog's name because I see this problem so often. I ring the doorbell, the dog starts barking and the owners are yelling at the dog to be quiet. When I walk in, the dog will jump all over me and the owners will be grabbing the dog, trying to pull it down, totally frustrated and embarrassed. We all know that dog!

This is one of the biggest complaints I get from owners. Again, every owner sets their dog up for failure. We just assume the dog will eventually listen to what we are saying, or else they will grow out of this phase. Sorry, but that is not going to happen. The dog's behaviour will only get worse. The dog is controlling this whole process, and because we are not communicating clearly to him, he'll continue to make the rules.

When dogs are making their own rules, they are controlling the house. On my first visit, I ask my clients what their rules for the house are. Most people have never even considered rules. They just believe you bring the dog into the home and he is going to be a great pet. As a family, you must have rules everyone will agree upon. You can't expect one person to follow the rules and the other people in the home to ignore them.

Mary and Molly

When I went to Molly's home for the first time, she barked when I rang the doorbell. When I went inside, Molly was bolting all over the place and hiding behind the owner. The owners tried to grab the dog, pick it up and pat her to reassure her. The owners just couldn't understand why the dog would react this way whenever someone came to the house. Molly had created a habit out of manipulation. She got rewarded (touched, picked up) whenever someone came to the door. Instead of ignoring the dog, the owners put all their attention on the dog instead of their guests at the door.

It took no time at all for the behaviour to continue to get worse because the dog always received attention from it. This little girl totally got what she wanted from the owners! To help Molly, leave her alone with all four paws on the floor, which builds confidence instead of creating more fear.

If Mary gives Molly attention only when she settles and relaxes on the floor, she will quickly learn this is the new normal. I am sure Molly reacted this way from the first time they brought her home, but if we react improperly or give attention to this behaviour, the behaviour will only get worse, which led to Mary's call for help.

Mat and Blaze

A nice family decided to rescue a dog that was around two years old. They had no previous experience with dogs but fell in love with Blaze when they met him. After having Blaze home for a few weeks, they noticed that when someone came to the door, Blaze would run up and grab the visitor's arm. He applied enough pressure to make their guests uncomfortable and this behaviour was making the owners nervous. I went to the home, and sure enough, the dog did the same to me. I ask the owners what they were doing to correct the behaviour. They hadn't made any corrections because they were afraid to discipline the dog, even though they were having no other issues with their dog.

We began the training program. Dad liked to run every morning and Mom walked the dog daily. The dog was pulling on the leash with Mom. You have to outsmart a dog if you want the dog to follow your rules instead of you following their rules. I taught Mom how to manage the dog on the walks and then we addressed the dog grabbing visitors' arms when they entered the house. Dogs just need to clearly understand what is expected of them. So here is what we did to solve this problem.

We leashed Blaze so he could drag it around the house. Then they could grab the leash and not touch the dog when we were working on correcting this problem. When a visitor entered the house and before the dog could get to the visitor, Dad would step on the leash, grab it up and then turn and walk the other direction. At this point he would drop the leash. If the dog went back toward the visitor again, Dad would go tie up the dog on a stair railing or door handle into a timeout. After a week of working on this behaviour, the owners finally found success and Blaze would lie down when someone came to the door because they would reward or touch him when he chose the right behaviour (lying down).

For some reason, this dog had created its own rule at the door, but no one had ever told Blaze he wasn't allowed to grab a person's arms. When Blaze began to understand the new rule and Mom and Dad consistently relayed that message, the dog made a better choice and received a reward — touch!

Conclusion

You set the rules, not the dog! If you don't, they will, and you won't like their rules. The reason most people hire me is because the dog is making up all the rules and the owners don't know how to manage the dog. Dogs thrive very well with rules. I have never known a good dog that didn't follow rules. Good dogs are good dogs because they understand their position in the family. The family creates the rules, everyone follows the rules and the dog is happy because of the rules.

Action Plan:

1) Follow the rules daily.
2) Everyone in the household must agree to follow the rules.

Measure of Success:

Is the dog following the rules? Are you and your family consistent with the rules? Can the dog *SIT* and *STAY* for 10 minutes waiting to be released?

If so, continue reading and we will work our way to teaching the dog *Down*.

CHAPTER 7

Don't Ask!

Charlie come, Charlie sit, Charlie, Charlie, Charlie...

And still Charlie is not doing what we are asking of him. Quit asking! Be clear and tell your dog what you want through body language. The martingale collar and six-foot leash is the best way to communicate with Charlie. When the collar is fitted right, you attach a six-foot leash and apply pressure to make the dog think through what you want, then release pressure when he does what we expect.

This is the only way dogs learn. Teaching the dog through his primary means of learning will go a long way toward a lasting result. Just like a bridle and reins for a horse, the collar and leash does the same for a dog. We need tools and our body language to help the animal to learn. People will argue this point, but I challenge you to try it. Grab a treat and ask the dog to sit. When the dog sits, give him a treat. Great!!!! Now ask the dog to sit with no treat. How well did that go? When you move with a dog, stop, draw up on the leash, apply pressure and he sits. Release within a short time when your feet stop moving and your dog sits.

I don't want to ask my dog. I want my dogs working for me and paying attention to me. I want my dogs to have a constructive job and mental stimulation. If I ask, motivate, and give eye contact, I am doing all the work and the dog is doing none. When I move, I want my dog to move with me and when I settle, the dog will settle. If we show the dog this is what we expect, they will do it. Praise with touch. They understand what we want.

George

When I first started out in my field, I took on a client and agreed to do the training myself instead of the owner. I would work with the dog four days a week and then on the final three days that week, the owner was instructed to follow the rules I had applied to the dog. I attached George to me for two hours daily and didn't talk to him. He got off-leash walks and we worked on all the basic obedience commands. I had George with me for six weeks.

During this time, through my body language, collar, and leash, I told George exactly what I wanted without words. Drawing up on the leash for a *SIT*, stepping on the leash when I wanted him to lie *DOWN*, turning my back on him if I opened my arms and he didn't come and always moving the opposite direction of the dog so George would stay in a proper heel position. At one point, I wanted to teach him that he had to *SIT* when he came up to the patio door from our backyard. When he stepped in front of the door, I would stand with my feet shoulder width apart and no eye contact. As soon as his bum hit the ground, I would immediately open the door. I have used this exercise on many dogs since then and it always works. Making a dog think through what we want for behaviour is so important!

I fed him a species-appropriate diet and we would play before he left to go home for the evening. Every training session was done in a new location, and all training was done outdoors with tons of distractions. Many times I would make him do exercises while other dogs were playing.

George was an excellent student. To date, if he is with me, I don't need to have him on a leash, and he walks in a perfect heel position. When I start to raise my leg, George will lie down. George loves to work and set a good example from which other dogs could learn.

I didn't ask. I told George what I wanted, and we have a fantastic relationship. Because I understand how dogs learn and then applied this knowledge to teach, this training session with George was a huge success.

Lucie and Shelbie

Lucie had a year-old Shiloh shepherd. She weighed 95lbs and the dog weighed 100lbs, so of course she was being dragged around. Week after week, nothing changed. Lucie catered to every one of her dog's needs. She let the dog drag her around, thought everything Shelbie was cute, and she couldn't understand how not talking to the dog and just telling (using the leash) her would or could make a difference.

During week four of training classes, the dog was walking with her. Shelbie listened, did all the exercises, and didn't drag Lucie. The dog's focus was on her. After class I asked what had happened to see such a change. Lucie had taken the dog out for a leashed walk and to practise exercises from the class. She lived on a farm, so she had lots of room to roam with the dog. At one point, Shelbie caught sight of a bunny and off Shelbie went — Lucie included. Because she had wrapped the leash around her hand, by the time she got loose she was scraped, bruised, dirty and totally frustrated. She walked home crying. The whole time, all she could think about was, "I can handle a horse, but not this dog."

Lucie had several horses and she worked with them daily, yet she couldn't handle a 100lb. dog. This is when she finally understood that she wouldn't allow a horse to treat her the way the dog was treating her. Her mindset changed from this dog being her baby to the dog being an animal.

Before she even attended the next class, she understood what I was saying, applied what she had learned and could now manage the dog. She no longer asks! If she wants the dog to *SIT*, she draws up on the leash and makes the dog *SIT*. If she wants the dog to lie *DOWN*, she steps on the leash. By the end of our training session, this brilliant dog was working with her. The dog's focus was on her and she could command the dog to do anything. This dog wanted to work for her, and she just couldn't see it until she applied the lessons. The respect for the dog and the dog's respect for her changed in 24 hours and they ended up being a fantastic team!

Lovable Lab!

A young man signed up for a group training with a 16-week-old pup. He was the most adorable chocolate lab ever! It was hard for everyone in class to keep their hands off the pup.

This owner took everything I said at face value, applied all the knowledge and worked on all the exercises. At 20 weeks, this pup could do a five-minute *SIT/STAY* in the core of our small town. Now, you want to talk about distractions. A class full of puppies, cars, people, trains and horns, and the smells alone could drive any dog crazy. The owner never asked his dog to do anything. Instead, he gave him clear instruction through the leash. He understood how to use the leash to apply exercises and make his pup do what he wanted.

Shortly after the session was over, the young man moved away. He continues to apply what he learned and sends me videos and pictures of all his adventures off-leash with his dog!

Conclusion

So yes, you can ask a dog to *SIT*, but why would you? Nothing is better than the privilege of having your dog off-leash and trusting your dog to behave off-leash. Teaching the dog to make good decisions and then allowing them to make good decisions is freedom for both you and your dog. When you really understand how dogs speak, you'll start to see your dog's behaviour in a different way. You'll develop friendship and trust with your dog. Your dog is always willing to defer to you instead of chasing that bunny.

I was at an off-leash park one day. I went there to observe owners and their dogs. Most people walked through the gate, let the dog go and then stood by the gate, spending time on their phones, chatting with a friend or sitting on the bench. No one seemed to care what their dogs were doing or where they were. Their dog with muddy paws could be jumping on a lady, humping a strange dog or worse yet, a person's leg., I was not overly familiar with big off-leash parks, but I was shocked to say the least.

One lady was getting ready to leave, so she started to prep her dog. "Buddy we're leaving in five minutes!" Then she continued to talk to her friends. "Come on, Buddy it's time to go now!" Still talking to her friends. "Damnit Buddy, I said it's time to go!" She then turned and continues to chat with her friends. I made a tick on the paper every time she called Buddy. She called 76 times. She finally decided to quit screaming and yelling the dog's name, walked through the gate, and headed back to her car on her own. Guess what? Buddy ran up behind her. So yeah, go ahead and ask. The dog got a clear message when she turned her back and walked away and quit asking the dog to come.

I took a group of five dogs (not all mine) to an off-leash area. I opened the door of the vehicle and the dogs jumped out. They followed me into the park, played as I walked around, then followed me out of the gate and back into the vehicle. Oh, and did I mention there were no leashes on the dogs, and I didn't talk to them. The purpose of an off-leash park is for the dogs to play and engage with other dogs. Standing around, talking on your phone, or ignoring what your dog is doing is not okay in an off-leash park. If you want to visit with a friend while the dogs play, keep moving!

Action Plan:
1) Don't ask. Use pressure and release to make your dog understand the command you are asking them to do.
2) Taking the time to allow your dog to think through the process of what we want. For example, waiting for your to dog sit outside the back door before you open the door is time well spent.
3) Challenge your dog. Longer *SIT/STAY* commands, more distractions and added distance. Move a leash-length away from your dog as you do the exercises.
4) *Down* is the next exercise to add to your commands for the dog to follow.

Down — With the leash attached to the dog and your hand in the handle, step on the leash using the leg that is farthest from the dog. Now step on the leash closest to the dog with your other foot. Step close enough to the dog so his head goes below the shoulder. Now just wait and let the dog think through what you are asking. When he lies down, wait until he relaxes before removing the foot farthest from him. If your dog starts to get up, step back on the leash. If he stays down, follow the same rule as you move the foot closest to the dog off the leash. Stand in the heel position and release the dog with the command, "All done." The leg closest to the dog moves first.

Measure of success

Do you notice your dog paying more attention to you? Does your dog yawn? This is an indicator of the dog thinking? How quickly does he lie down? Once the dog goes down as soon as you start to apply pressure on the leash, use the command, "*Down.*"

CHAPTER 8

Change, No. Consistency, Yes!

Over the years, I have had a hard time getting dog owners to understand you can't change training methods based on what is happening in your life, if you don't believe the dog is responding to the training methods, if you're tired of doing the work involved with a pup or you just want to try something new and different. The poor dog will be so confused. This type of change is NOT good for your dog. I know because this is exactly what I did with my own two dogs — Mason and Brady. I changed training methods daily and couldn't understand why nothing was working. My poor dogs were so confused.

Did you know the dog's learning development happens until the dog is three years old? During this time, the dog goes through several growth spurts and changes. You need to be consistent with your method of training during this time to ensure you'll have a well-mannered dog.

Change is good, but not in the way most people think. Change the time of day you feed your dog. Change where you walk your dog. Change the time of day you play with your dog. The purpose of change here is so your dog is always looking at you to see what is happening. Dogs learn to be patient while waiting.

Sometimes we get into patterns and routines in our lives out of convenience and sometimes out of boredom. When routine happens, your dog may become bored with life as well, and that can create problems. If you do the opposite of what a dog wants, they will eagerly await your next move. I know this can be difficult with your own work and life but try to the best of your ability to change things up for your dog. Dogs get little stimulation in their lives — food, water, walks. Try changing things up to add a little excitement to their day.

From a client's point of view, consistency is feeding time, feeding the same food daily, walking the same block around the neighborhood on a leash, waking up at the same time every day or three walks a day. Clients often believe this kind of consistency is good for the dog.

From my point of view, consistency looks like this. Dogs must *SIT* every time we enter or exit a home. My dog must walk in a heel position when on a leash. He must lie down when I step on the leash. He must come when called. My dog must be checking in with me often. He must stay or wait when asked. Whatever command I give my dog, he must do it the first time! I will continue to work on this until my dog fully understands what is expected of him. It is so cool when you realize your dog totally understands your expectations.

At the age of three, Reba finally goes to the front door, lies down, crosses her feet, and waits patiently for me when I am getting ready to leave the house. That was a long time coming! She only got rewarded when she lay with her feet crossed. Now she does it all the time just so I will tell her she is a good girl and give her a pat!

Frank the Mastiff

Frank was 180lb mastiff. He was a great family pet with one problem. He liked to jump on everyone! Grandma weighed 100lbs and the wife was pregnant at the time. This was becoming a problem and of course they were worried about the coming baby. For a dog that would listen to all his other commands, this problem just didn't make sense to me. When I arrived at the home I found out that Dad loved for the dog to hug him. Well, now it all made sense! They had rules for everything else except jumping on people. Frank was allowed to jump on Dad, so it wasn't surprising that he thought that went for everyone. The owners thought it was fun until Grandma got hurt and Mom was pregnant.

When I arrived, I stood very tall with my shoulders back, feet apart and no eye contact with Frank. The owners couldn't believe the dog didn't jump on me. Then we had Grandma enter the way she normally would enter a room and the dog jumped. Then I worked on her body position and we tried again. The dog didn't jump. Now all they had to do was to be consistent in their body language, setting the rule for no jumping ever, and incorporating a consequence of "time out" if the dog didn't follow the new rule.

Dad was not happy. He loved that his dog hugged him, yet he could understand why Frank was jumping on everyone and that he had created the problem. So I explained that Dad could have whatever behaviour he wanted with Frank, but he had to "invite" the dog. Dad taught Frank that when he patted his chest, the dog was allowed to jump up. Within a short period of time, the dog understood what we wanted.

Dragging a leash while in the house gives owners the ability to manage the dog when someone comes to the door. This tells the dog, without touch, they are not allowed to jump. They called a few months later. Their baby boy had been born, the dog hugged dad on command and Grandma was no longer getting pushed over. I love these stories. Consistency always wins!

Angie and Mat

A young schoolteacher had rescued a dog. She was in love! He was a wonderful dog and I could definitely see why she rescued him. Although Mat behaved well on many levels, Angie couldn't get to the point of trusting the dog. We started to work together.

After a couple of weeks, the problem became obvious to me. She wasn't consistent. We'd wander around her neighborhood working with the dog. Angie would move, and one time when she stopped she would make the dog *SIT*, yet the next time she would forget and not put the dog in a *SIT*. Sometimes she would let the dog lead and then she would get frustrated and make Mat walk in a heel position. She had a hard time understanding that if she consistently made the dog *SIT* every time her feet stopped, the dog would *SIT* whenever her feet stopped.

Handling a dog needs to become an automatic habit. She really believed that if she worked on things here and there, she would get to the point of trusting Mat, but dogs need to have clear, unwavering expectations!

Conclusion

As you can see, consistency is the winner! Consistency makes sense to a dog. They don't want to be confused. They just want to know what is expected of them. That is why I love dogs so much. Rules are love to a dog. Structure is love to a dog. Expectations are love to a dog. Consistency, rules, structure, and expectations equal LOVE from a dog's perspective.

Action Plan:
1) Be consistent in your expectations of your dog. Your dog must *SIT* at the door when coming in or going out. Your dog must lie *DOWN* on its bed while you eat supper. Your dog must walk by your side when it is on a leash. Your dog is not allowed to rush to the front door when someone arrives and will only be touched when all four paws are on the ground.
2) Train with higher distractions.
3) Work on keeping your dog in a *SIT/STAY* while you move farther and farther away and with lots of distractions.

Measure of Success:
    Does your dog *SIT* every time you walk to the front door? Is your dog willing to obey even when you apply distance and distractions?

CHAPTER 9

Food Matters

Years ago when I started down my path of working with dogs, food was brought into the discussion as part of a dog's healthy life. I was raised a farm girl and we had dogs over the years that ate our leftovers or kibble. I had no idea how much the type of food could affect a dog mentally, physically, socially, and nutritionally. So one of the first things I did when my first level of training was done was to research dogfood.

I had two shelties at the time, and both were constantly at the vet's office. Itchy ears, diarrhea, constipation, smelly ears, bad breath, and their coats were a mess. They had dry and brittle coats that were difficult to brush. Then there were their teeth. At five and three, their teeth were already yellow with tartar build up. The vet suggested we do an expensive dental surgery within the next year to get the tartar off their teeth.

I had no idea that by feeding a species-appropriate diet, all these problems would go away on their own. I have since learned, like kibble, there is a wide range of raw food available for sale. But they are not all equal. So, I followed my gut and chose a product that was produced under one roof, made with local ingredients and designed by a canine nutritionist. Within three months I could see huge changes in my dogs. They no longer had bad breath, the itchiness went away, there were no more smelly ears and brushing them had become a simple part of our routine. Because they now had the proper oils in their skin, they did not shed as much, if at all, and there was no more painful matting. The tartar on their teeth broke away when I gave them raw bones to chew on.

The best part was their poop, which used to be HUGE, runny, smelly, and just plain gross! You can imagine what a problem that was with two shelties! Now I can pick up the poop with two fingers. It doesn't smell and it is about the size of a thumb.

What an eye-opening experience this was for me. So I continued to educate myself about the relationship between dogs and food. I contacted the company three months later and have offered raw food to all my clients as another part of my product line and as a healthy lifestyle for their dogs.

Carlos the Bulldog

A woman contacted me about a dog she had recently acquired. Carlos was around two and he had huge patches on his sides that were dark, almost as if the hair was dying, and he was refusing to eat. She had visited the vet with Carlos, but nothing seemed to be working, so someone suggested she call me. I took a case of raw food out to her home. As soon as I opened the car door, the dog wanted to jump into my car. I pulled out the case of raw food and opened it up, then gave the dog a frozen patty. Carlos wandered onto the grass, ate the puck, and came back for more. Three months later, the patches on the side of his skin were gone, he was at a healthy weight and ate his meals regularly.

Shelley and Mickey

Mickey was a raw-fed dog, but he suddenly refused to eat his food. The owners were going away, and they were concerned that Mickey was sick. Shelley stopped by my house to discuss raw food. I gave her two pucks of my product and suggested she try that before going to the vet. She was back in five minutes. The dog had eaten the pucks frozen and wanted more. As I said earlier, not all products are equal, and dogs have a great sense of smell. Their nose tells them when they shouldn't eat something. We will never know why exactly Mickey decided to quit eating a particular raw food, but what I do know for sure is my dogs have eaten the same product for nine years and have never refused to eat.

Missy (food)

I hadn't worked with Missy and her owner long before they decided to feed raw. All of Missy's other needs were being met. She had off-leash time daily, she attended several training sessions of mine, both group and private, and was fed raw.

Missy is a German Shorthair. Anyone who knows this breed understands how active they can be. Missy prefers beef in the summer because it is lower in fat and keeps her body cooler. Then she'll eat chicken in the winter because it has a higher fat content, which keeps her warmer. Missy eats little if the weather is hot or she doesn't burn a lot of energy on a particular day. She may eat a whole bunch if the weather is cold or if she runs far and fast.

Her owner understood not to leave food lying around, not to give Missy tons of treats and to let the dog tell her what she needed. Missy will bark for food and she will receive one serving. If she barks for another serving she will get it. When she quits eating one particular food in the spring or fall, the owner knows it is time to change her diet. Missy may eat as little as one serving a day or up to six servings a day. It all depends on the time of year, how much exercise she received that day and what the temperature was outside. Not all dogs will self-regulate, especially if there are other dogs in the home, but Missy has always done a great job!

Brady

Brady is my Shetland sheepdog. He prefers beef. I started him on raw at the age of three. At that time, I was visiting the vet on a regular basis, but as I mentioned earlier, after feeding raw, the vet visits ended. When I explored how important food was to a dog's overall health, I continued to educate myself about species-appropriate diets. . Brady only wanted to eat the beef. If I tried any other protein, he would eat it if another dog was around, but if left on his own he would only eat the beef. So I trusted that he knew what was best for him and I fed him beef.

I learned many years later that a dominant dog needs the strong smell of beef to let other dogs know he is the dominant dog. Gus, who I spoke of earlier, will only eat chicken. He's a submissive boy! Gus doesn't want any attention given to him, so he wants his smell to be light. Mikka eats according to season and amount of exercise she gets.

Brady had TPLO surgery on his back leg. A few weeks after surgery, he broke the bone under his plate. He ended up in a crated area in our home for eight months. The reason I am telling you this is because I learned how important it is to have a pup come from a mother who was fed raw and a grandmother who ate raw. The farther down the line the female eats the right diet, the stronger a dog's internal and external bodies will be. This is what builds strong and healthy bones and bodies in dogs. Feeding raw will go a long way toward the health of your dog, but a puppy coming from a raw-fed mother is even better.

For the eight months Brady was in his crated area, he could not be groomed. When he was fully healed, we went to the groomer. Although his coat was a mess, the groomer said she was surprised at how nice his coat was to brush out. Years earlier, I had difficulty brushing his coat when I brushed it daily!

Conclusion

Food is a huge part of the health of your dog. As with humans, if we don't eat whole, living, raw or fresh food daily, we will see and feel a difference in our health. Throughout history, dogs have never had a full bowl of food lying in front of them all day to eat whenever they felt hungry. The forest didn't have kibble. Dogs have had to roam until they found food (mice/rabbits/grass) or were given scraps from our tables.

If allowed, dogs will self-regulate how much and what kind of food they want to eat. Allowing a dog to self-regulate works with one dog in the home but it will not work if there are two or more dogs. If one dog is having a hard time eating, I will put another dog in the room to ensure the first dog will eat. To keep our oldest dog Mason eating, I would feed him close to Brady. At the end, he quit eating and I knew for sure it was time for him to pass on.

Keeping your dog at a healthy weight is important. Less is more. We can all relate to the most current information coming out about overall health for humans. A healthy weight is always best for us, and fasting is a big thing today and shows some amazing results in humans. Yet dogs have done it for years. Dogs naturally fast when they are sick, and so do we. We don't eat when we are sick and yet we get upset when our dog doesn't eat. If your dog is fasting, trust that there may be something going on. Allow them 24-48 hours to feel better. Make sure they have access to water at all times. If they are still not eating after that time then it is time to visit the vet.

FOOD MATTERS! Take the time to learn about the benefits of raw food for dogs. Do your dog a favour and feed a species-appropriate diet.

Action Plan:
1) Learn all you can about a species-appropriate diet for canines.
2) Buying treats for your dog is not necessary. Give them a piece of carrot or banana.
3) Daily whole, fresh, living food or raw food is great nutrition for your pup. It is nature's vitamin pill.

Measure of Success:
   Is your dog excited to eat? Can you feel the dog's ribs but not see them?

Here are the important points we've learned:

1) You need to be a confident leader for your pup.
2) Teach your dog. Don't react.
3) Consistency will always win in the end.
4) Tools are an important part of the dog's ability to learn. Use a martingale collar and a six-foot leash.
5) The dog should have four paws on the floor at all times.

6) Body language is the only way a dog can gather information about you or another dog.
7) Create a calm environment and your dog will learn to be calm.
8) Exercise, training, nutrition, and socialization create a well-mannered dog.
9) Touch is the only reward a dog needs for a job well done.
10) Be more fun for your dog than anything else in the dog's life.
11) Pressure and release on the martingale collar is clear communication to your dog.
12) *SIT* — Remember, each command needs to be done 10x daily for a total of 200-1000 reps for the dog's full understanding. Every dog learns at a different rate. Track progress on a calendar.
13) Drag a leash in the house so you can interrupt behaviour you want to manage in your dog. For example, four paws on the floor instead of jumping on the couch.
14) Rules/Structure/Expectations equal love to your dog.
15) *SIT/STAY*
16) House rules: create the rules, abide by the rules, consistently ask the dog to follow the rules.
17) Create five household rules for the dog and write them down.
18) *DOWN* – 10x daily for a total of 200-1000 reps.
19) When the dog has a clear understanding of the command, add time, distance, and more distractions. Remember, a dog will always do what is asked in your home. Challenge the dog outdoors to complete commands.
20) Food matters! Try to feed your dog something whole, living, or raw daily.

We have covered a lot of information up to this point. Building up a dog's confidence and trust takes time and energy. Many people want to skip important steps in working with their dogs, but like building a house, you need to start at the bottom and work your way up. Dogs learn the best in the first three years, so take your time, teach the dog until they completely understand what you are asking and then move to the next level of training.

Dogs may be smart and learn quickly, but until you can ask a dog to *SIT*, and they get no body language clues from you, treats or hand commands, the dog does not completely understand what you're asking.

My story about Reba going to the front door, lying down and crossing her legs without being told and her consistently doing this on a daily basis means she understands what I want from her. With her lying at the front door, I'll open the door and command, "Load up." She'll immediately run to the back of my car and jump in. I got Reba at 16 months and she was around three years old when she started doing these behaviours on her first ask. CONSISTENCY will always win!

Now it's time to move forward. Let's take your dog to the next level!

CHAPTER 10

Confident Manager

Leadership, dominance, and boss are words used to make people think they are managing their dogs. These terms refer to the opposite of positive reinforcement. Some people choose to view these words as good while some view them as bad. I choose to use the word *leader*. Let's explore what the word LEADER means and then you will understand why I chose this word.

1) *Clarity* — They are clear and concise — there is no mistaking their expectations.
2) *Decisiveness* — They don't hesitate to commit. They show great consistency with their decisions, rarely backing out or changing their minds unless it is absolutely necessary. Being decisive shows commitment to the process of learning.
3) *Courage* — To do the right thing.
4) *Passion* — They love doing what they are doing.
5) *Humility* — A leader is always ready to learn, grow, admit when they did something wrong and teach what they believe is right.

If I am my dog's leader, it is a working relationship that is good for both parties.

Very few dogs want to be the leader, so that is why it is so important that we are good leaders for our dogs. They understand when we clearly communicate, make quick decisions and are consistent with our expectations.

Missy (training)

Missy warms my heart, but she was the hardest dog with whom I have ever worked. She was a German Shorthair that was not going to be used as a hunting dog. Many people entered Missy's home on a daily basis. Although the owners wanted a well-trained dog, they never achieved consistency. No matter what we worked on, someone would come in the house and undo any progress we had made. The owner had clear expectations but no one else respected her rules for the dog. Not surprisingly, Missy was confused! The owner continued to work with Missy, apply the rules and be consistent. I learned lessons about so many things with Missy. Not all breeds are the same or should be treated the same during the training process. You may think your dog is not learning, but he really is!

Hattie contacted me by phone to inquire about dog training. She told me she had a six-month old female GSH and wanted to understand more about my training methods. We met downtown for some private lessons. Molly was goofy and silly and just wanted to play. She was soft and gentle and had a big heart. After a couple of weeks of training, things were not going as planned, so I agreed to take Molly and do some work with her on my own.

Training was extremely difficult. I spent many hours frustrated with not getting results. Even when I did have a good session with Molly, the next time we met, I felt as if I was starting from scratch. Molly was socializing a lot with people but not with other dogs. She'd had no off-leash runs and no mental stimulation prior to starting with me. I reviewed everything I knew about training at the time and read books on German Shorthairs, but nothing seemed to work.

One day I was so frustrated I just threw the leash over her back and started walking away from her as fast as I could. The next thing I knew, she was walking right beside me. We walked downtown for 1 ½ hours with the leash dragging on the ground. She would *SIT* at every corner, stayed right by my side, and followed every command I asked her to do. I realized at that point that I didn't understand how smart she really was. I was treating her like a baby instead of a dog. She had truly learned everything I had taught her, but because I wouldn't let the leash go, she could never prove to me how much she had learned.

What was going on behind the scenes to make training so difficult? Many people entered and exited the home daily who did not follow the rules Hattie had put into place. This created much stress in their home. Molly was not being run to burn off her stress and energy. She was being fed a kibble diet and had no dog friends.

Between private lessons, group lessons and my own work with Molly, over the next several years, she achieved great results. Everyone said Molly would never change and Hattie would never be able to trust her. We proved everyone wrong, and for years now I use Molly to help me demonstrate how a well-mannered dog behaves. It was a slow process with lots of ups and downs, but I taught Hattie about dog behaviour and what Molly needed to become a loving companion. Hattie learned how to trust Molly, and now they have a relationship based on mutual respect.

We could not control what other people did, but we put in place rules and expectations and continued with training class. Hattie and Molly attended agility, rally obedience and many of the pack walks I offered. All of the changes gave Molly the mental and physical stimulation she needed. Hattie started on a species-appropriate diet and only used treats of the highest quality. Hattie got to meet some new people and have fun at classes with Missy. Attending fun classes such as agility or a rally go a long way to relieve stress for both the dog and owner. Socializing with people of common interests is good for us and our dogs.

Hale and Dingo

Hale and his wife attended group training. Dingo reacted to everything! Dogs, people, the leash, wind. Everything set this dog off. Hale constantly reassured the dog with touch. Because my training was all done outdoors, there was always something setting off Dingo. Each week we would meet somewhere new which always took Dingo out of his comfort level. After the first class, I instructed Hale to walk with his dog around the outside of the group. He had to keep moving and he was not allowed to touch the dog unless the dog sat and was calm. At that point he could reward with touch.

He could have no pressure on the leash, and he had to give the dog the entire leash. Whatever direction the dog went, he was to turn and go the opposite direction. For this group training, we met two times a week for six weeks. In the last class of the third week, Hale and Dingo could finally join the group.

With my training approach, Hale learned very quickly that he'd created the problem, and had been reassuring Dingo there was indeed a problem by touching him whenever he was stressed. Hale had to learn to move quickly, make decisions (instead of second guessing everything he did), be clear with his expectations and have the courage to be consistent so his dog could learn. By the end of the six weeks, Hale and Dingo had an amazing new relationship and Dingo was a great family dog!

Clair and the Poodle

A young single mom got a poodle. The dog was out of control. The older the dog got, the worse the problems became. She could not trust the dog off-leash. The dog bolted every opportunity he got, and he jumped on everyone. Mom was so stressed because no one wanted to be around her or her dog anymore. Clair was unable to manage her dog. He was spending most of his life in a kennel. Week after week, she saw no positive progression with the dog. Mom just could not be the **leader** for the dog. On many occasions, I would take the dog and work with him. The poodle responded great when I was handling the leash. From that, I knew the dog would and could learn, but Mom just couldn't do it. She finished her lessons no further ahead with her dog than when she'd started. I recently heard the dog bit a child. How sad! Training can be difficult but is totally worth the work and time spent.

Conclusion

Dogs need a leader. Otherwise, they can get into trouble. Fake it until you make it! I use this quote constantly. Standing tall, learning how to handle a leash, and giving the dog the leash instead of you reacting or getting stressed is important! Managing a dog is not about being mean or hurting or dominating your dog. Managing your dog is about your confidence — trusting yourself and the dog.

Action Plan:

1) Work on your leadership skills.
2) *DOWN/STAY*

DOWN/STAY — The same as the *SIT/STAY*. Now ask your dog for a *DOWN/STAY*. Work up to 10 minutes and then with distance and distraction.

Measure of Success:

Put your dog in a *DOWN/STAY* in a downtown location of your city or town.

CHAPTER 11

Scared Stiff

Dogs react and give warning before they bite. Whenever your dog makes a bad decision and bite, the dog warned beforehand, and the bite was done with intention because the dog was not taught to make a good decision. Don't make excuses for him because this does not fix the problem. You may have created the problem, but your dog made the choice to bite. You are not doing yourself or your dog any favours by making excuses. Get busy, clear up the communication and have expectations for your dog.

Dogs that make bad decisions such as biting are confused, and most of the time, although not always, we have created the problem. When the dog gets to the point of biting, we need to explore and learn about this dog so we can determine why the dog bit. Was it the owner or was something else going on with the dog? A vet health check is always first on the list to ensure the dog is physically healthy. Aggression in dogs is complicated and it takes time to determine what is going on and what aggression we are dealing with. I rarely have these cases. Poor behaviour or choices usually come when the mental, social, physical, or nutritional needs of the dog are not met. Sometimes, the dog just needs to be told the behaviour is not acceptable. I have met several people who don't take dog bites seriously. A bite is serious and should never be ignored, whether the dog is five pounds or 100 pounds. You must immediately act to help this dog and change the behaviour.

Della/Peter and Sam

In order to change dog behaviour, you must teach your dog to make good decisions, which means they need to be invited on furniture, beds or to jump on people. Dogs that make their own decisions are not trustworthy.

One time, I was asked to go look at a pup, under a year, because the dog would bolt every time the door opened. When I arrived, Sam barked so much that we couldn't even have a conversation. He was peeing in the house, and he didn't even know what a collar and leash was. The couple invited me into the house. We went into the kitchen and I was invited to sit at the table. To my surprise, the dog peed on the table right in front of me.

Well, I knew this dog was out of control and would require a ton of work to change Sam's behavior. Whenever we tried to have a conversation the dog would constantly demand attention from the owner. She said Sam would pee or bark every time she got busy making supper. This dog had no rules, no expectations, and no leadership! Thank God, Sam was young, and we could train him. Sam had been allowed to create all his own rules in the house and the owners didn't know what to do when he did something wrong, so they just didn't do anything but give him attention, which inadvertently rewarded the behaviour. Therefore the behaviour got worse!

This dog had not bitten anyone yet, so it was important that we started training with him immediately. Incorporating commands, leashed walks and dragging a leash in the house gave Sam an understanding of how he was expected to behave. Simple solutions created a balanced dog. A few months later, they had a dog they loved and enjoyed. They got lucky! Many times, the story doesn't end happily.

Steve and Bear

A young man contacted me because his dog had bitten him, and he just couldn't understand what was going on. Sometimes when we rescue a dog, we believe if we love him enough nothing bad will happen. He loved his dog so much!

When I got there the dog was so good. He was quiet, listened well and appeared to be a perfect fit. But Steve couldn't go anywhere with Bear. As soon as he took him outside, fear set in and the dog reacted to everything.

This was an older dog, so the chances of changing behaviour were unlikely. He explained to me that he had been trying to get Bear outdoors and to go for walks. One day, a neighbourhood dog walked by their home.

Bear went crazy, and when Steve pulled back on the leash to try and calm the dog down, Bear ran back and bit him on the leg.

I continued to work with him weekly and then he continued on his own. The dog ended up bolting after a vehicle and was run over. Aggressive behaviours may be deceiving and "love" won't fix them. Dogs that bite are scared, confused or possibly sick. These dogs require extreme protocol (a strict training program) to change their behaviours, with lots of time, patience, and professional help. After years of strict training, some dogs go on to lead happy healthy lives. What took years to develop (fear, lack of confidence, no ability to trust) in the dog takes time to rebuild.

Andy and His Pack

One day, I was volunteering at a barbecue in our community. A man requested some of my time. He looked sad, so I stepped aside to chat with him. Andy lived in a small community and owned several dogs. He wanted my opinion on his dogs' behaviour. His friend had come over to the house a few days ago, and while they were visiting on the living room couch, one of his dogs had attacked his friend.

The man had a serious wound on his arm and went to the hospital for stitches. The owner said the dog had been teased by this gentleman in the past, and his friend wanted the dog euthanized. The more we talked, the more information arose. Andy had several dogs in his home. He kept them locked up in separate rooms because all they did was fight. He would take turns taking the dogs outside on a leash for their bathroom breaks. Recently, this particular dog had started chewing through the wall to try and get at the other dogs.

He continued to tell me none of the dogs were fixed, all the dogs in the house were siblings and all were under three years old. He had never allowed the dogs to socialize with other dogs. They had no outdoors time other than on a leash to pee and the dogs were only used for breeding. My heart was breaking! Then he rolled up his sleeve. His arm had been completely shredded. The dog that bit his friend had also attacked Andy about six months earlier. There wasn't much left of his forearm. I told him this was beyond my expertise and I referred him to a behaviourist for the proper evaluations.

I am not a behaviourist, but what I do know for sure is these dogs problems got worse due to lack of socialization, a lack of exploring the world off-leash, lack of basic obedience training, lack of leadership, lack of friends and lack of quality nutrition.

All these years later, this case and many others are reminders of how bad some dogs' lives end up. Locking up your dog is taking away his life. Some dogs need professional help, and not all people have the time or patience to be good dog owners. These stories break my heart. All these dogs are all examples of fearful dogs, which are the most dangerous. Any time I hear of a dog that bites, it's heartbreaking.

Conclusion

When we give our dogs the option to make bad decisions, that is on us and we need to fix the problems. Start with basic obedience training, be patient and continue to work with your dog for as long as it takes to build confidence and trust. If your dog is truly aggressive, you'll need a behaviourist to help you create a plan based on the type of aggression your dog is displaying.

Action Plan:

1) *COME* 10x a day until you have completed the 200-1000 asks.

COME — If you have brought a pup home, whenever he looks at you, open your arms wide. When your pup runs into your arms, get excited and play with him. If he doesn't come to you, ignore him, turn your back and walk away.

If you have adopted a dog, remember to build the house. Do all the commands listed above first. Once those are completed, place your dog in a *SIT* and *STAY*. Pivot in front of the dog, and as you back away, drop the leash out in front of you. When you get to the end of the leash, open your arms. If the dog gets up before you ask him to by opening your arms, place him back into a *SIT*. If you have followed all the commands above, your dog should know by now how to do a solid *SIT* and *STAY*, which means he can't move unless you release. If your dog stays in the *SIT* position, squat down, open your arms and tell your dog to *COME*. When he gets to you, ask him to *SIT*, grab his collar and then reward with touch. If he doesn't move, pull on the leash, place the dog in a *SIT* in front of you, grab HIS collar and reward with touch. Repeat.

During the years of working with clients, I have commonly seen dogs start to *COME*, but then they bolt as they get close to the owner. This becomes a game which you must nip in the bud. *COME* means for your dog to come to you and *SIT*, and then you'll grab the collar so you can manage him if necessary. Or *COME* means the dog must be close enough to you and you are managing the dog. *COME* does not mean bolting to avoid touch. You ought to have the ability to put on a leash.

Add more distance and distraction if your dog is on the path of good recall. You can use a 25' lead to manage the dog when you add distance or distraction. This will give you the confidence to manage him if he does decide to bolt while in training.

COME is the command that is most wanted and useful by owners. Unless you understand dogs, do the work (build the house), meet the dog's needs and teach him not to react, you will never have a reliable *COME* command.

Measure of success:

A young couple hired me to help with their new pup. She was pregnant and they wanted a reliable dog to be a part of their family. When we started working together, I noticed very quickly the dog's *COME* command was perfect. This couple understood the importance of getting excited and welcoming the pup every time he ran into their arms. They were happy with good energy. If the pup didn't come, they ignored the wrong choice. I must honestly say the dog's recall is still 100% to this day. Is your dog's recall 100%? If not, keep working on the command. It takes time, good energy, and consistency.

CHAPTER 12

Quit Apologizing

As I have said, I have heard it all! My dog doesn't like men, my dog doesn't like men with hats, my dog doesn't like people with glasses, my dog is scared and that's why he pees in the house, my dog has predatory aggression when he sees a rabbit, he's just protecting me, he's a German shepherd so he naturally protects, he's just herding because that's what they do, my neighbor's dog is crazy so my dog chases the fence, my dog doesn't like to be outside, my dog prefers my bed so when he gets mad I sleep on the couch, he's just excited to see you, he won't bite...

Don't apologize for your dog. It's better if you understand your dog so you really know what is going on. Some men stand tall, have deeper voices, and move with purpose, and that is why the dog reacts. I often do the same when I enter a home and hold the same body language as a man.

Dogs react to people's energy, so your dog could be reacting to nervousness with the man wearing glasses or a hat, or maybe you are scared of the man. How much attention are you giving your dog when they react to the man with the glasses?

When a dog is given the choice to chase and has been taught to not pay attention to the owner, they will chase. A dog should take all its directions from you. Have you ever seen a police dog not focused on his handler? Every herding dog I have ever known is given instructions on what they should do. You can't be responsible or manage anybody else's dog, so work on managing your dog instead.

Bad manners and bad behaviour is never a good thing when it comes to a dog that can move way faster than any human and they only have their mouth with which to protect themselves.

Emily and Max

Emily had a beautiful German shepherd. Emily rescued this dog at a young age. He was two and she had little dog experience. Emily loved this dog and couldn't understand why he reacted to everything. I agreed to start working with her. Max weighed around 75lbs, while Emily was not a very big girl. She was young, soft spoken and let the dog drag her around.

When we met, she apologized for every bad decision her dog made. She wanted to walk the dog but was too scared to let him off leash. She said Max was scared of people and other dogs. I invited her out to one of my group classes. She was required to have the dog on a leash when she arrived and to have the dog muzzled. She walked the outskirts of the class hoping the dog would relax so she would then eventually be able to join the group. Close to the end of class, we let the dogs off-leash. Her dog went into flight mode and started to run back to her car. I told her to ignore him and continue walking with me. A few minutes later, the dog was walking alongside us.

I told her to continue to ignore the dog and just let him figure out what he should do. The dog never engaged with any of the dogs, but at least he didn't run away. He was quite nervous. I had also instructed everyone else in the class to ignore the dog. We did this exercise a few more times and Max finally started to adjust to people and dogs. Then summer came along, and she decided not to continue working with me. She thought Max just needed to learn to socialize with other dogs and as long as he got to run with other dogs he would be fine. She didn't want to believe there are many other components of working with a dog.

In the fall, she met up with me again. Now the dog was charging at me, still not biting, but we were headed in that direction. She truly believed "love" was all the dog needed, so she still wouldn't let the dog run off-leash (unless I was there), she had done no basic obedience (mental stimulation) and other dogs had still not learned to be with other dogs because she didn't want to put a muzzle on Max and let him run with other dogs.

Emily believed because the dog was a German shepherd, his job was to protect her, so that is exactly what the dog was doing. Emily touched the dog constantly, and because she was nervous, the dog felt the need to protect her. The touch was the dog's approval that he was doing exactly what she wanted. Working breeds need to work! You can give them a constructive job to do, but Emily didn't want to manage the dog.

Apologizing for this dog's behaviour did nothing to help Max. Sad case! He is now tied up all day, every day, because she can't trust Max and she can't relax enough to teach him.

Kathy and Nik

Nik was Kathy's first dog. When she called me for help, Nik was growling at people, he would charge at people and he had no recall. He was running the show and Kathy had no idea how to change what was going on. I spent so much time laughing because Kathy would apologize for every behaviour Nik displayed. Kathy was amazing and I will always remember her as one of my favorite clients. When I arrived at their home the first time, Nik was growling, as she had stated. It took no time at all for me to realize the problem was not Nik, it was Kathy.

As I have explained, most things with dogs are counterintuitive to what humans think and this is where all of Nik's confusion came in. When Nik growled, Kathy didn't know what to do, so she stood there and petted him to comfort and reassure him. Nik also got too close to the front door when people entered and exited, which made Kathy nervous, because she was afraid Norman would bolt. So after we chatted for a while, we began to work on the door issue. Within no time, Nik understood he had to come to the end of the railing and stop, sit, and wait for further instructions.

Nik had tons of off-leash time and had friends to play with every day so the only thing we had to work on was his confusion with his owners. He did quite well at commands, but only when he wanted and not necessarily when they asked. Nik needed structure, rules and then love. He was spoiled and they knew it!

After doing weekly lessons, Kathy signed Nik up for a group class so he would have to deal with bigger distractions. Nik had to learn to be invited on the couch, to jump up on the husband and do whatever command was asked the very first time. Nik now makes good decisions and has the best life ever! There are so many dogs that get to a point of "running the show," and then are handed back to the shelter. Nik was lucky his owners chose to learn and teach instead. No more apologizing necessary!

Dawn, Peter and Lucy

A nice couple hired me to help with their dog. When I went to the front door, complete chaos ensued inside the house. Everyone was scrambling to grab the dogs, who were all barking. I was instructed not to come in until the dogs were put away or leashed because they would bolt. I was not to touch the oldest dog because he would bite. Boy, did I have my work cut out for me! The endless apologies started the moment I got into the house,. All the dogs in the house had been rescued. But because they were "rescued," each dog had sad stories attached. I ask the couple how well the stories were working for them? Obviously, not well! They proceeded to tell me their routine and schedule so all the dogs could be in the home together. I was shocked. I had no idea that dogs were so much work. I told them our goal was to have happy, healthy dogs. These dogs needed to act and function like dogs.

The oldest dog was just old and grouchy, so there was nothing we could do about that. But the other two were immediately put into training. No beds, no couches, no talking, and the owners were only allowed to touch the dogs when they did the correct behaviours we wanted. When we took the youngest dog outside, he went crazy, so I asked the couple to sit in chairs on the front driveway and hang onto the leash. Every time the dog laid DOWN, they were to touch the dog and tell him he was a good boy.

A week later, I walked up to the front door and there was no chaos whatsoever. I walked inside. The dogs were lying on the floor in the living room except for the youngest, who had decided to jump on me. I continue to work with the couple for many weeks and they, too, joined a group session to expose their dog to new dogs and to work with lots of distractions. To this day, I see the couple out walking with their dog on a leash and he is happy and healthy.

Conclusion

You can apologize all you want for a dog, but if you want the behaviour to change, you need to get busy and teach your dog how he should act! I have never seen any apology work to cure a behaviour. In fact, it will make the behaviour worse.

Action Plan:
1) Don't apologize. Understand your dog's behaviour or understand how you are contributing to the problem.
2) Don't touch or give your dog attention when they are nervous. Continue to move. When the dog shakes off the stress, reward with touch.
3) Love will not fix problems.
4) Walk with your dog on a loose leash.

LOOSE LEASH WALKS — Owners create so much bad behaviour in dogs because they won't take the pressure off the leash or drop the leash so the dog can explore the world with no restrictions. You've seen dogs dragging their owners down the street or a dog lunging at the end of the leash. If you apply pressure on a leash and continue to do this, over time, your dog will eventually react on the leash. GIVE THE DOG THE LEASH! At no time should there be pressure on the leash. This is an easy correction to make. When the dog hits the end of the leash, turn and go the other way. Don't pull back on the leash! When your dog is pulling from the side or behind, move faster. When he is walking in a proper heel position, reward with touch. Your hand should only be in the handle of the leash, which automatically makes the leash loose, allowing your dog to move and think. Every time you pull back, don't release the pressure or wrap the leash around your hand, you are telling your dog there is a good reason for him to be stressed. Then the dog reacts, and you no longer trust the dog, resulting in the dog not getting leashed walks.

Measure of success:
   Do you apologize for your dog? Can you walk your dog with only two fingers on the leash?

CHAPTER 13

Clever K9

Almost daily, clients will ask, "Why does my dog _____?" My reply is, "Why do you let them _____?"

You must be smarter than your clever canine. Dogs move faster than any human, they are masters of the human body language and they know how to manipulate humans to get or do what they want. Most experts agreed a dog is about the mental age of a 2.5-year-old child. In my mind, the reason a dog appears smarter is because he has mastered human body language, giving him the ability to manipulate a human to achieve the results they desire.

Pay close attention to your dog's behaviour. If, or when, you are with multiple dogs and people, watch what the dogs will do. Dogs will run to the person they believe will give them attention. This person usually stands softer, has a smooth tone of voice, may have a smaller body and will often bend over toward the dog. All dogs will run over to see who can get the attention first. Then watch how a dog will react when a big strong man marches along. The dog may cower a bit, stay away or run up behind the man to sniff. It doesn't mean the dog is afraid. It just means the dog understands that this man is confident and a leader, so the dog will show respect. No dog will compete for this man's attention, because he knows he will get attention when the leader is ready to give him attention.

Mindy and Jake

Mindy rescued an 18-month-old Border collie two years ago in the spring. She lived on a farm and spent most of her days outside. Mindy was out one day in the fall and heard a gun fire. Hunting season had started. She continued to do her work, and when she turned around Jake was headed for home. Border collies can be known for timid behaviour around unknown noises or situations.

We started with all the basics, attaching the dog to her, and teaching basic commands, but most importantly, I taught her how to handle a leash. One exercise she had to do was head out on a leash walk when she saw or heard the hunters. When a gunshot went off and Jake tried to bolt, she was to take off running in the opposite direction. The only time Jake was to get a touch reward was when he made the choice to stay with her instead of bolting.

When the next hunting season came along, Mindy called me to say she could have Jake off-leash when she was out working in the field. The following year, Jake had no reaction at all to the gunshots.

If Mindy would have given attention or excuses instead of building the dog's confidence, Jake would have gotten worse, and I am sure, like many stories go, he would have gone missing one day. Teaching a dog to take directions from you will pay off. Help your dog by being smarter than him.

Jimmy and Gus

Jimmy and his new dog Gus joined one of my group training classes. Gus was a hunting dog, so he was good with his nose and would rather smell than listen. During class, the owner would continually pick up the dog. Gus was allowed to block Jimmy's movements, he would run between Jimmy's legs, jump on him, and bite the leash. Jimmy would get frustrated and walk off to the side of class to let the dog sniff and smell.

Class after class, the dog continued with this behaviour because he got rewarded with doing what he loved, smelling the grass. On many occasions, we talked about how dogs manipulate owners, pulling on the leash, blocking the human, running between legs, jumping, and biting the leash. Dogs can only do what is available to them to get the results they desire. This dog was making all the decisions and the owner allowed the behaviour to continue. Gus won the battle.

The owner could not see the behaviour as manipulation. Jimmy had every excuse — the dog was tired, or we didn't get the dog out for some off-leash time or Gus was too young to learn. By the end of the six weeks of training, the dog cried like a baby whenever another dog came near him, which resulted in Jimmy picking up Gus. Jimmy felt the other dogs were picking him. If Gus was on the ground and another person came near Gus, Gus would growl, and Jimmy would get nervous and touch Gus. Gus was under a year old and all this behaviour was developing because the owner was not smarter than the dog.

Here is a case where you have a perfectly good dog, but because the owner is not acting like he is smarter than his dog, this dog will develop behaviour that could lead to a bite, at worst, or bad manners, at best.

Kathleen and Bailey

Kathleen rescued Bailey at around one year old. Kathleen had no previous dog experience, so she brought Bailey home, let her sleep in her bed, didn't do any obedience training, allowed Bailey to only run off-leash and play with other dogs and watch TV on the couch with her. Kathleen had a crate for Bailey but thought it wasn't fair to put the dog in a crate.

After a year, Bailey was showing undesirable behaviour to the point where she bit a guest in the home, so she rescued another dog, hoping the dogs would play and be tired and therefore not bite. Surprisingly — not really —

the dog bit again, and this time it was much worse. Finally, she decided to call me.

This is another situation where Kathleen was not being smarter than her dog. Bailey was rewarded with more of the things she wanted every time she performed a bad behaviour. The dog was now around 2 ½ years old with two bites on her record. Kathleen had a boyfriend, so training began with both dogs at the same time. Bailey had to wear a muzzle when they were out of the house and I would not enter the house unless Bailey had the muzzle on. These dogs' lives were all play and no work.

They decided to sign up for six weeks of training. They were asked to connect the dogs to them for two hours daily, put the dogs in crates when they were away from home and place them in a *SIT* and *STAY* for everything. The dogs had to stay on the mat when they were eating supper and were no longer allowed on couches or beds. The dogs needed to learn that they must take direction from the owners, not make their own decisions. Off-leash play was allowed after they had completed all their exercises for the day. As the weeks went on, both dogs showed great progression, barking had been reduced and the dogs stayed in a proper heel position instead of blocking the owners with their bodies.

By the end of the six weeks, you could actually knock on the door with no reaction from the dogs. Although they came a long way in six weeks, the owners had to continue with training. When a dog is allowed to make all the decisions for 2+ years, you know have to change the behaviour you've created and that takes time, commitment, and patience.

Conclusion

If your dog has a behaviour you don't like, don't allow it! You must be smarter than your dog. Then, you must be consistent during the training phase to teach the dog to change the unwanted behaviour. On many occasions, I have lacked staying consistent with my dogs and I, too, needed to go back to training. Many people tell me they can't make their dog sit, yet in the same breath they will say, "I insist my dog sits for food. We can't have our dog aggressive when food is around." If dog owners would insist their dog behaving in all situations, they wouldn't have a problem with their dog in the first place. Be smarter than your clever K9, set up rules and apply the rules until they become a habit for you and your dog.

Action Plan:
1) What do you need to do to outsmart your dog?
2) When your dog performs a behaviour you don't like, teach your dog and change the behaviour.
3) Be consistent!
4) Teachers don't react.
5) Reward the behaviour you desire through touch and, "Good boy."
6) Insist your dog behaves in every situation.

SIT/STAY/DOWN/COME/LOOSE LEASH — Complete all commands in high distraction areas of your city or town.

Measure of success:
Time, distance, and distraction is your indicator of how well your dog training is progressing. The longer your dog will *SIT/STAY, DOWN/STAY*, up to 30 minutes, it means you have done the work and most likely have a very well-mannered dog. Keep up the good work!

CHAPTER 14

Train Daily!

I could talk about dogs forever. More stories, lots of laughs, so many different breeds, so many different personalities, training, sports, and the list goes on. Talking about dogs, reading about dogs, and watching TV programs about dogs will not change any bad behaviours in your dog. As much as you think learning different methods of training may help your dog, isn't true. What really works is picking one method and applying what you have learned. Just do it! Make up your mind that training is important. Incorporate training into your everyday life instead of as something extra in your already full day.

Dragging the leash on the dog gives you the ability to grab the leash if the dog does something wrong. Connect the dog to you for a couple of hours daily. Cutting the grass, vacuuming the house, washing clothes, reading a book, doing dishes, or working on your computer are all good suggestions. Draw up on the leash and make the dog *SIT* every time you enter or exit the home, get in and out of vehicles or go up and down stairs. Place the dog on a mat or bed and make him *SIT* or lie *DOWN* while you cook supper. If your dog gets up, simply place him back in the same position.

Open your arms to invite your dog to *COME* whenever you notice your dog looking at you. Take him for an off-leash walk. When he is busy playing with other dogs, call your dog to you. If he doesn't *COME*, turn your back and walk away. You need to be creative! Put your dog in a *SIT/STAY* while you have a phone conversation. Make your dog lie *DOWN* on the front step as you load up your car. Tie the dog to a fence as you move around. Hide from your dog and then call him. Make your dog jump up over any safe object (outdoor table, large rocks, etc.). Connect your dog and weave through a row of trees. You and your dog will have so much fun! Touch and movement are so important for your dog. Get moving and get excited. Touch or play when the dog does what you want.

Holly and Blue

Holly brought home a mini Australian shepherd. This is a breed Holly had her eye on for years and she'd finally purchased her dream dog. Although she'd attended many dog-training classes and lots of off-leash pack walks, she'd never applied what she learned. Holly had read tons of books, watched many programs on TV and watched YouTube videos, but Holly only wanted to learn. It really doesn't matter how much you know or understand about dog training. If you don't apply the exercises or teach your dog, nothing will change. Holly's dog cries whenever another dog comes close to it. Blue can't maintain a three-minute *SIT/STAY*, the dog won't *COME*, and the dog still won't lie *DOWN* on command. When asked if she'd done the homework from the previous class, she always had an excuse. Holly made lots of time to chat about dog training but never applied the lessons.

Trevor and Shelby

Trevor rescued a pup from a local shelter. Shelby was four months old and Trevor was excited to start training with his new dog. Trevor did tons of research online, but by the time Shelby was a year old, she was out of control and he was having a hard time managing her behaviour. Trevor would spend hours trying the clicker method and command/treat but nothing worked.

Trevor joined the class and challenged every aspect of my methods of training. He never understood that he needed to pick one method of training and be consistent with the method he chose. He would come and do a class with me and apply my methods, then go home and use treats, then the next day try the clicker again. This poor dog was so confused. You have to pick the method of training that works for you and then be consistent with that training. Dogs learn at different rates. Just because you don't think something is working doesn't mean it isn't.

Most dogs need to apply an exercise at least 200-1000 times before they completely understand your expectations. If you change training methods daily, your dog will be confused.

Sarah and Bindy

The first time I met Sarah and Bindy was in an, off-leash park. Bindy was a doodle, and the pup was out of control, to say the least. Bindy would pee everywhere, spin in circles, get in all the other dogs' faces and jump on dogs and people. Sarah would just sit, watch, and laugh. Sarah had no idea how to handle the dog. She was nervous and allowed Bindy to do whatever she wanted.

The dog had begun to aggressively chase vehicles. When Sarah heard I was a dog trainer she was willing to sign up for some classes to see if she could get this behaviour under control. When I handled the leash, Bindy would do whatever I wanted her to do, but as soon as Sarah held the leash, Bindy was immediately out of control. Sarah didn't actually want to do anything to train her dog. She only wanted to listen and watch everyone else learn the exercises.

This dog now has two bites on her record and never has any off-leash time. Bindy continues to chase vehicles, which at some point will end her life. Another sad case which could have been resolved with daily training and clear expectations.

Conclusion

There are a lot of great dogs out there that require little training. We have all seen, owned or heard of these dogs. However, the majority of dogs need direction, rules, expectations, consistency, training, movement, leadership and management. You must make a plan when you decide to be a dog owner and then get busy and do the work required to have a pet you can take with you no matter where you go. If you are creative, you will find a way to train as part of your day, not as another thing to do in your day.

Action Plan:
1) No excuses!
2) Incorporate training into your day.
3) Connect the dog to you while you make supper/cut grass/watch TV.
4) Make your dog *SIT* for everything.
5) Ask the dog to *SIT/STAY* while you talk on the phone, load up your car, send a text, write an email.
6) Ask the dog to *DOWN/STAY* while you make supper/wash dishes/work on your computer.
7) Work on leash skills while going for your daily walk.

Measure of Success:
 Are you creative and thinking of ways to mentally stimulate your dog while doing your regular daily tasks? Does your dog move with you outside or around the house and then settle when your feet stop moving?

CHAPTER 15

Party Time!

Even though most dogs only mature to the age of a 2 ½ year old human child, they have a brain and we need to make them use it. When you require a dog to use his brain, they need much less physical exercise. One indicator that your dog is using his brain is yawning. People think the dog is tired, but he is stimulated by something going on around him. You will commonly see a dog yawn when they are performing basic obedient exercises. After teaching a group of pups for 30-45 minutes and then allowing them to play for 20 minutes, you will see the result long into the next day. It is worth your time and effort to teach your dog basic obedience, increasing time, distance, and distraction to make the work mentally harder.

Karen, Her Doodle and Friends

Karen and her friends hired me because they were concerned that the only thing their dogs would do was play. They couldn't separate them, and the intensity of the play was increasing the likelihood that one of the dogs would get hurt. This group allowed the dogs to play instead of making them work first. Just like anything in life, too much of one thing isn't usually very good for us, let alone a dog. This is what happened to these dogs. Life was all about play! There were no boundaries, no rules, and no leadership, and even though these pups were young, and most people would think they should only play, all dogs need structure.

After only a few lessons, the dogs learning to work first created a safe environment for the dogs to play. The level of play came down a notch, there was more respect between the dogs and the play didn't last as long.

Go sit at an off-leash park and watch the dogs interact. As you watch, you'll notice some dogs that you will question whether it is play or on the verge of a fight. This is common behaviour you will often see in off-leash areas because owners use the off-leash area to burn off the dog's physical energy, but it does nothing for his mental energy.

Before entering an off-leash park, take your dog for a walk and make him complete some basic obedience exercises. Stimulate his mind, get his attention, and follow the most important rule — work before play!

Harold and Pack

Harold loves dogs! He started with one and signed up for some training. He did okay, working with his dog, but Harold was a softy and really couldn't understand why he had to train his dog. Dogs are just love. He wanted his dog in bed with him, and he just wanted to take his dog to the off-leash area to run and play with the other dogs. Even though he did some training, he was never consistent, so the results were minimal. His dog had no recall, couldn't *SIT* on command, and absolutely refused to lie *DOWN*. The dog was chewing up everything in his home and jumping all over people.

Less than a year after getting this dog, Harold decided to get another dog. In his mind, the dogs would play all the time and then they would be tired, and all the problems would go away. The problem with this thinking is that an ill-mannered dog teaches another dog ill-mannered behaviour. A well-mannered dog teaches another dog good behaviour. So now he had two bad dogs, so he registered for another set of training classes and enrolled both dogs. Nothing had changed. HIs dogs were still in bed with him, he wasn't consistent, and the dogs just wanted to play.

The most shocking part about this story is he got a third dog and history repeated itself once again. Now he is that guy in the off-leash park who everyone avoids because he has three ill-mannered dogs. If you don't teach a dog to use his brain, if you don't stimulate his brain, nothing in the dog's behaviour will ever change.

Conclusion

I have spent many hours with dogs that have jobs and use their brains, and there is no comparison to those dogs that are just allowed to play. Most people say, "Well, I have a huge backyard." That's good, but it is not enough for most dogs. Yes, dogs are social animals, but like us, all play and no work usually doesn't end too well.

A dog at one year old is comparable to a six-to-seven-year-old child. At that age, your child is going to school, has chores, has new friends, and is required to do a bit of homework. Most people believe a dog at a year old is still a puppy (baby). By the time your dog is eight months old he will be going through his "Terrible Twos." Training should start anywhere from 10-16 weeks. By 16 weeks, your dog has already acquired tons of information about you and will have started the manipulation.

Action Plan:
1) Dogs should always work first, then play.
2) When you release the dog from a leash after training, use the command, "*GO PLAY.*"
3) Start using multiple commands. *SIT/DOWN/STAY/COME*....
4) Give your dog a job, a sport or rally obedience to keep the mental stimulation going once you have completed this dog training program.
5) *WAIT* — getting out of a dog's sight builds confidence.

WAIT — Unlike *STAY*, *WAIT* means the dog can sit, lie down, or stand as long as it stays in the place you've told the dog to *WAIT*. Start by placing the dog in a *SIT/STAY* with you in the heel position. Tie the leash to a pole, fence, or whatever is available. With the palm of your hand facing down and in front of the dog's face, tell the dog to *WAIT*. Walk away with your back to the dog. Move around and practice getting out of the dog's sight. If the dog stays in the *WAIT* position, go back and reward with a touch saying, "*GOOD WAIT.*" Apply more distance and higher distractions as the dog understands the purpose of the *WAIT* command. If the dog starts to make any noise, go back and say, "*NO NOISE*," with meaning and purpose, then, "*WAIT*," and walk away again.

Measure of Success:

Can you go to your local coffee shop, put your dog in the *WAIT* command and go grab a cup of coffee? Can your dog do multiple commands?

CHAPTER 16

In the Habit of Getting ATTENTION!

We think our dogs need all our attention. When we enter and exit the home we give our dog all our attention. When we sit on the couch we cuddle the dog. When we go to bed, the dog comes with us. We spend time walking the dog, playing with the dog, talking to the dog, looking at the dog and allowing the dogs in our bed. More dogs than ever are struggling with inappropriate behaviour because we are using the dog as our comfort, our security blanket, and our way to relieve anxiety.

There is nothing wrong with this if the dog is actually trained to be a therapy dog or a service dog. Dogs that are actually trained to help humans are amazing and do a great job for many people, but don't expect to have a therapy dog when you actually brought home a companion dog.

When we do the things I mentioned above, without first training, we confuse the dog because he doesn't have rules, structure, leadership, and expectations. Attention can be a form of manipulation. When a dog demands attention such as walking in front of you, lying on your feet, sitting on you when we you on the couch watching a TV program, pushing another dog away or making you touch them before you greet your partner or children, the dog is controlling the environment, which to that dog is sending a clear message to other dogs or people that they are the top dog. The pup that pushes the most when he is with mom is the fattest.

Dogs learn very early on in life what they have to do for food or attention. Dogs that get so much attention struggle when left at home alone, do not do well in a crate and destroy many items around the house. They are known to struggle with appropriate behavior toward people and dogs and don't have good manners.

Spoiled Sally

Sally is your typical small dog that is never expected to put four paws on the ground, explore the world, spend time in the crate and worst of all, doesn't socialize with other dogs or people. I have seen Sally hundreds of times. When I arrive at the house, the owner is carrying the dog around, the dog is barking like crazy and baring its teeth and is snarling and snapping. She won't stay on the floor and the owner won't make the dog sleep in a crate. The owner has hundreds of excuses why the dog behaves the way she does.

My first question to each owner is, "What would you be doing if this dog weighed 100lbs?" Owners respond with, "Oh I would never allow that to happen." So why do you allow a small dog to behave like this? Most people never make the connection that a 10lb dog is no different than a 100lb dog. We tolerate bad behaviour from small dogs but have zero tolerance with the identical behaviour in a 100lb dog. It is so easy to pick up a small dog, travel with a small dog and have a small dog in your bed or on the couch, but creating bad behaviour through too much attention is never good, whether the dog is small or big.

Sherry, Mason and Brady

Yup, that's right, it's me! Chaos happened every time I would enter or exit the home. After I left my day job and our dogs got my attention all day every day, they would bark, jump, and shake toys whenever I entered or exited the home. I would encourage them. I loved my dogs being so excited to see me. Until I understood dogs, I didn't even realize I was creating so much stress for our dogs, and the more time I spent with them, the more they barked and jumped. The daily chaos was getting worse. During my training, I was challenged to enter and exit the home giving the dogs no attention until they laid down and relaxed. Well, guess what? All of a sudden my dogs were calm.

The dogs learned very quickly that they received attention for calm behaviour not excited behaviour. This was one of the most eye-opening experiences for me. Dogs react. When they get attention for that reaction, the behaviour gets worse. I had to learn to reward good behaviour and ignore the bad. I only touch the dogs when they are doing the exact behavior I expect or when they are relaxed and calm.

Touching a dog when you are nervous, or the dog is nervous, puts a lot of stress on the dog. Now when I know a dog is stressed, I continue to walk with the dog. At some point the dog will "shake off" the stress. Only after the dog has released his stress will I give him any attention.

Karen and Jesse

Karen had a Lab named Jesse. Jesse was a great dog, but when Karen went for a walk, Jesse would lunge to the end of the leash when another dog got too close. Because Jesse was around 60lbs, Karen would wrap the leash around her hand, make Jesse sit and constantly rub her hand down his head and tell him it was all right the other dog wouldn't hurt him.

On our first walk together it was apparent that Jesse felt the need to protect Karen. Jesse was alert and stressed when we got outdoors. He constantly blocked her movement and sat on her feet in front of her. Karen's frequent touch reinforced to Jesse he was doing exactly what she wanted him to do or needed him to do. At one point he was baring teeth at me, and she continued to touch him, which again reinforced the behaviour.

We started with basic obedience so I could see whether she was allowing that leadership role to begin. Karen worked hard and Jesse was doing well. We met at a park one day and I instructed Karen to let Jesse hit the end of the leash when a dog went by. She was to take off running and call Jesse by name. If he ignored the other dog she was to reward with play! Within a short period of time, Jesse was relaxed and sitting on the grass with Karen not reacting to any dogs walking by. She would reward him with touch if he stayed lying down with no growling, barking, or lunging. Jesse was quick to realize the attention he got for the good behaviour was better than chasing after the dogs.

Karen will need to continue working with Jesse on this exercise for a long time to ensure they develop a new habit of being calm around other dogs. Dogs need to be rewarded through touch for good choices. Jesse was that dog that made everyone nervous or afraid. He looked vicious! He was stressed, yet when Karen learned about touch and movement, things changed. The dog learned he could "shake off" his stress, relax and get attention for good choices!

Conclusion

When given at the wrong time or place, attention may confuse your dog. This is the biggest problem I see on a weekly basis. The dog then will make bad choices, which causes us to react by touching. The next thing we know, we have a dog we can't trust. Attention for good choices results in a confident dog with reliable recall, calm energy and who is a dog you can trust! Touch and movement are two of the most important training concepts owners need to understand. Get in the habit of rewarding good behaviour instead of bad. **IF YOU DON'T KNOW WHAT STATE OF MIND YOUR DOG IS IN, DON'T TOUCH THE DOG!**

Action Plan:
1) Touch the dog when he is making good choices.
2) When your dog is stressed, don't touch. Rather, move until the dog shakes it off.
3) For 24 hours, no touching, no talking or looking at your dog. See how hard he works to get your attention.
4) "*ALL DONE*." Teaching the dog to release is an important part of training.

ALL DONE — When a dog is in the heel position, the leg closest to the dog should move first. This indicates the dog can move. Once we add the words SIT/DOWN/STAY and the dog is doing the commands on the first request, then as the leg closest to the dog moves add the words *ALL DONE*. As the dog's confidence builds, when you get to the point of having distance and distraction, commanding the dog *ALL DONE* is the next step. If the dog doesn't move, stand beside the dog, then release with your leg moving while you say, "*ALL DONE.*"

Measure of Success:

How long does it take your dog to settle? Does the dog wait patiently for the next command? Does your dog move when you move and settle when you settle?

CHAPTER 17

A Dog's Tale

If you listen to and watch a dog, they will tell their story. When I do group training or work in private, the dog tells me whether the owner has done the work, if the owner applies consistent rules and if the owner set high expectations for the dog. I don't need to ask the owners what they have done. I watch the dog.

You will see results in 24-48 hours if you apply what you have learned, have no excuses, allow the dog to be a dog and quit giving him so much attention. Dogs reacts to everything we do. When we understand that our dog is reacting to us and change what we do, the dog will settle into the new way of doing things. For example, if when we're nervous we then coddle the dog, the dog becomes stressed and reacts.

When I come into a home, I instruct the owners to ignore the dog and let me see how he reacts. Each home is different, and each dog tells a story about that home. I won't give eye-contact or touch the dog and I keep my body language soft. I talk to the clients while completely ignoring the dog. Some dogs become very stressed, some stare at me, some go hide and others just go about their lives as if nothing is going on. Although the majority of training is the same for most dogs, how quickly we move through the lesson and what homework each client receives is always different. When we need to build trust or when a dog is highly stressed, we slow down the process.

Jake, Carol, and Ally

A young couple called to start training with their one-year-old golden retriever. When I arrived, the dog was doing whatever she could in order to get my attention — running in circles, whining, and constantly wanting in or out of the house. Ally could not settle at all. Even though the couple gave the dog daily exercise, played with her and socialized her with other dogs,

Ally would not relax. Why? Because the dog constantly received touch for bad behaviour.

We added basic obedience exercises and a species-appropriate diet. They were the proud parents of a baby girl, and Mom was exhausted and stressed because the dog wouldn't settle. Mom really didn't want to have to add one more thing to do in her already busy day. The dog slept in their bed, but the baby had her own room. Daily, Carol would walk the baby in her stroller and take the dog along. Ally was about 55lbs and hard to manage with the stroller. After three weeks of training, nothing had improved. There was no consistency and no time to train the dog. Ally was still receiving touch for bad behaviour. With the high level of stress in the home and a lack of training, Ally nipped a lady who entered their home.

Now the stress level was even higher, and Mom wanted to get rid of the dog. Ally truly believed it had to control all of its surroundings, which was too much stress for a dog of this age. The dog was always trying to let the owners know she was stressed, but the owners didn't know what to do to help the dog. Ally didn't want to be the leader, but she would step up if no one else learned how to manage the dog.

So here we start small. No touch unless the dog is calm. Talk to the dog as little as possible, making the dog pay attention to you. The dog must *SIT* for everything, giving the dog some mental stimulation.

Because the dog was so stressed, and we needed to build trust, we moved slowly through the training program. We gradually added more commands. The owners had to learn not to touch Ally when she was stressed.

Months later, Jake and Carol invited me to their home. They had a calm relaxed dog that no longer demanded attention. The family will always need to be aware of when and how much attention they are giving Ally. The dog needed her space and they needed theirs, so they crate trained, so Ally had the option to go to a safe space. And they needed to continue with physical and mental challenges. If at any time this couple goes back to old habits, the dog will, too.

Molly and Max

Molly joined a class with a rescue pup around six months old. She was excited to get started with training. When she arrived at the class, Max was crazy, jumping, excited and not paying attention to her at all. This is quite normal behaviour when you put a group of dogs together on the first night of training.

We began class, and as time moved on she got farther away from the group. She was wrapping her leash, was frustrated, and was trying to calm Max down through talk and touch. As you know by now, this just makes things worse. She attended three classes and then quit. She called me to explain why she quit.

Although she wasn't afraid of her dog, she was afraid of other dogs. The dog was completely reflected her fears, which could set in motion bad results for her dog. Lack of socialization, Molly's nervousness, no obedience training, and a lack of movement will not set this dog up for success.

Action Plan:
1) Understand why you are touching your dog. Only touch the dog when you are calm, and the dog is calm.
2) A dog needs his space and you need your space. Crate your dog so you and the dog can have a break when needed.
3) Listen to your dog so he can tell his story! When a dog does something you don't like, most likely he is reacting to something going on in his life.

CHAPTER 18

Good Clean Fun

Now that we have spent the time and energy to teach our pups, they are willing to obey, have good manners and we are much more knowledgeable about dogs as a whole, let me help you navigate a couple more things.

Dog parks may be fun for dogs, but you must be on the watch at all times to prevent any injury to yourself or your dog. As a dog owner, you should know what to do and how to approach a dog fight. People jump in the middle to break up fights, and many get injured as a result of breaking up those fights. I will give you tips to help you make an educated decision as to when and how you break up a dog fight.

We all would like our dogs to visit a dog park and have fun. When dog owners don't understand the body language of their dog or don't make it their business to keep moving and pay attention to the behaviour of their dog, both dogs and people can get hurt. Here are some guidelines to follow when visiting an off-leash park.

DOG PARK RULES:

1) This is the place to socialize your dog. IT'S NOT FOR EXERCISE. Do not bring a high energy dog to an off-leash park. Get the zoomies out before you socialize your dog.
2) Watch the dogs in the park before you enter with your dog. Make sure there are no dogs present who are displaying inappropriate behaviour. Your dog's safety is always #1.
3) Remove your dog's leash before you enter the park.
4) Only enter an off-leash park if your dog obeys the *COME* command 95% of the time or better.
5) YOU must be the leader.
6) Carry your leash so you have the option to leash up and leave if necessary.

7) If YOU can't be calm, then don't enter an off-leash area.
8) Don't bring toys or treats to an off-leash area.
9) It is your job to pay attention to your dog's behaviour. For the safety of your dog, pay attention to the other dogs, as well.
10) Dog parks are NOT about human socialization. Continue to move while in the park.
11) Do not allow your dog to mount another dog or another dog to mount your dog.
12) Uncontrollable barking can be irritating to some dogs. Leave if your dog won't quit barking or if another dog is barking too much and you notice the dogs are getting irritated.
13) Don't let your dog chase joggers, skaters, or cyclists.
14) If children are screaming and running around, I will either leash my dog until things calm down or I will leave (high-pitched noise is stressful to a dog).
15) Don't talk to your dog. Your dog must have four paws on the ground at all times. The purpose of going to an off-leash park is for the dog's social needs. It's entertainment for the dog.
16) Do not bring a female in heat, or pregnant, or a mom and her puppies, to an off-leash park.
17) Do not bring your dog if it shows signs of aggression to other people or dogs.
18) Healthy dogs only!
19) Dogs should be vaccinated and spayed/neutered.
20) Don't forget to pick up after your dog and dispose of the waste in the garbage on your way out.

Let's look at some of these comments a bit closer. We rush home from work, grab the dog and, with only an hour before we head home to make supper, we need to let the dog burn off some energy. Other than bathroom breaks, the dog has been home alone during your work hours. When we are stressed, in a hurry and on a schedule, the dog is, too. Before you enter an off-leash area, walk for a couple of blocks, do some basic obedience exercises, and have a bit of fun with your dog. Your focus will be on the dog, which will help you clear your energy from the day at work. And your dog will focus on you. After you have the dog connecting with you, then enter the off-leash park.

Your dog's safety is number #1! We all may believe we are only responsible for our own dog, but in truth, we need to watch all the dogs in the park to keep our dog safe. Watch what is going on before you enter the dog park, and then if all the dogs are playing nice, enter. If not, go somewhere else. Choose a new location or another off-leash park. You can always just go play with your dog or put the leash on and go for a walk. As stated earlier, changing things up for your dog is always a good thing. New location, new smells, new friends!

Some people leave a leash dragging or leave the leash on until they are in the park. I have seen leashes get tangled, which could lead to a dog fight, or a leash will wrap around a person's leg and pull the person over, or the leash gets caught on a tree stump or under a bench. Dogs run fast and play hard. This is not the place for a leash.

Your dog might not have 100% recall, but your dog's recall with distractions needs to be good. If you see something happening that could be dangerous for your dog, you will appreciate that your dog will recall on the first ask. Remember, *COME* means the dog comes to you, sits, you grab the collar and then reward with touch.

If you truly are the leader, the minute you head toward the gate, your dog will follow. That really is the best. I can be out with many dogs, and when I change directions, the dogs follow. Because I am the leader, I rarely, if ever, have difficulty with a dog not following my lead.

Carrying a leash needs to be a solid rule for you to follow. Whether you are at a dog park, at a friend's house with your dog or camping, when your dog is around you, carry the leash. You never know when a situation may arise, and you will need to leash your dog. Over the years, I have walked in many off-leash areas with my dogs. Coyotes, bunnies, or thawing ponds may require you to put a leash on your dog.

If you are uncomfortable in an off-leash park, don't go. When you are nervous, so is your dog. You can always practice spending time in an off-leash park. Take five deep breaths, make no eye contact with other dogs, let the other dogs smell you and keep moving. Start by entering the park for five minutes. Build on the amount of time you spend in the park as you get more comfortable. Most off-leash parks can be a great form of socialization for you and your dog.

A dog does not need toys or treats at an off-leash park. This is the place the dogs play with each other. When you are with a group of strange dogs, you don't know if these dogs have aggression related to food or toys. Toys and treats can trigger behaviour that is not appropriate in a dog park.

Your job while in the dog park is to move, watch what your dog is doing, and watch what all the other dogs are doing. If you feel other owners aren't paying attention to their dogs, there is too much barking going on, the play is too rough, a dog is overexcited while humping another dog or children are running around screaming, you may decide to leash your dog and leave.

I have seen parents encourage their dogs to chase the children. This is not an appropriate behaviour in a dog park. When children run and scream, some dogs may go into prey drive. I do not encourage any parent to let this behaviour happen. One day I was in an off-leash park and this small dog screamed because he got scared as soon as the owner set his paws on the ground. All the other dogs immediately ran toward the dog. The dogs believed this dog was injured. In this particular situation, if the owner hadn't picked up the dog, I am sure one of the other dogs would have killed this dog. Another big learning moment for me. If I had not yelled in a deep voice, something would have happened to the small dog. A situation escalated in less than five seconds. All 20 dogs were going to get involved. Don't ever forget that your dog is not a baby. They are animals!

I go on daily walks with my friends in areas where our dogs can be off leash. These walks are for the dogs, but it is a great social time for me, as well. I prefer this to a dog park. The dogs have tons of room to roam, we have spectacular views and we all get the health benefits of movement. In these wide-open spaces, the dogs may play a bit, but they mostly entertain themselves. I find in off-leash parks most of the dogs only play. There is not a lot of quality exercise or movement. This type of movement allows the dogs to relieve toxins from their bodies. I notice my dogs pee and poop way more when we are on these walks as opposed to an off-leash park where movement is limited.

Understanding Canine Body Language will help navigate the off-leash park:

1) When a dog places his neck and head over the top of another dog's shoulder he is saying, "I am Alpha!" Either the bottom dog will spin and say, "Let's Play" or will leave and not engage. When the top dog applies pressure on the bottom dog's shoulder, you will notice the tension rising. The dogs' bodies get tight. I recommend you interrupt the dogs. If another dog is stalking your dog, leave the park.
2) Not all dogs like each other. If your dog comes and stands behind you, respect your dog's decision and leave. We don't always see everything that is going on.
3) A play bow is always good — bent knees, open mouth, tongue out!
4) If there is a bully in the park, rolling the other dogs over, mounting other dogs, nipping other dogs, etc., I will leave if the bully is picking on my dog.
5) A small dog with a squeaking bark and quick movement can switch on the prey drive in other dogs.
6) When your dog is paralleling another dog, this is mutual respect. Let them run and play!
7) Let the dogs sniff nose to bum. Interrupt nose to nose interactions if the dogs' bodies get tight. Tension may be building.
8) Don't let your dog charge another dog. This is rude.

9) When you think the play is getting too rough, intervene and get moving. This should keep the dogs happy.

CHAPTER 19

Be A Smart Fighter

Have you ever been around a dog fight? It is scary. Lots of noise, fast movement, and blood, and we are left unsure as to what the best plan of action should be for the dogs and ourselves. Most of the time we just react, which is not always the safest way to handle a dog fight. I would like to give you some tips to consider. I know exactly the moment we are in a difficult position and need to make quick decisions.

I know we all want to break up that dog fight, and it is natural just to respond instead of thinking things through. My hope, by sharing some insight on dog fights, is that you will consider this information and then make a smart decision as to whether you should break up the fight or not.

1) Maintain your safety first.
2) Do you have experience breaking up a dog fight? If you are going to get hurt, stay out of the fight.
3) Who is the aggressor?
4) You need to make lots of noise, loud and deep.
5) All dogs move faster than humans. Your hand or foot will lose!
6) Do you know both dogs?
7) Is one breed larger than the other?
8) How big are you in comparison to the dogs? Are you strong?
9) Is the surface slippery?
10) Do the dogs have a leash attached? Are they tangled or can you grab one?
11) Do not scream in a high-pitched voice. A high screech can mean pain and may aggravate the situation. Again, loud and deep.
12) Do not put any body part between the two dogs.

Dog fights do not typically last a long time. Once the fight is over, remove your dog from the area. Stop to find out if any injuries have occurred and determine whether the dog needs to be seen by a vet. This is a very scary time for both dogs and people, so be careful! You don't want to do anything to reignite the situation. Be safe!

CONCLUSION

My Story!

This entire book was written from my personal experience. My clients (the dogs) have taught me so much over the years. Throughout the years, I found myself thinking of my childhood and what it was like to own a dog at that time. When I visited farms, I saw dogs settled and content. I began to realize that a life for a dog was so different years ago and because of these differences, our dogs sometimes struggle.

Dogs are carrying too much stress because of these differences. Not all farm dogs have a great life and I am not saying just because a dog lives on a farm they have the best lives. What I am saying is dogs today deal with so much more on a daily basis and we need to help them to live their best lives. Most of the clients I have worked with over the years are dogs that live in a town, their owners work many hours and the dogs live in homes. None of which is bad. It's just we need to teach our dogs how to handle all these differences. Dogs from years ago were left outdoors, stayed at home, had no toys and were not given constant attention or talked to all day. They didn't have to listen to children screaming, us fighting or loud TVs or video games. It is not the dog's fault.

It's more than basic obedience! Obedience is the simple part of dog ownership. We need to know and understand body language (both dog and human). Our dogs need to have friends and they need to run daily to burn off any stress they have acquired while being in our homes during the day. From my experience, dogs with jobs do well. We need to give our dogs a life with meaning and purpose — their job!

Our dogs deserve balance in their lives with a calm, confident leader. They need a species-appropriate diet because most of what we eat today is processed food, just like kibble. Anything that is processed lacks nutrition. When we eat whole, raw, fresh foods, our health improves, both physically and mentally. Well, it's the same for dogs. If a dog had to find its own food, he would eat mice, rabbits, grass, etc. Place a bowl of kibble on the floor next to a bowl of extra lean hamburger and see which the dog chooses to eat. Dogs live through their noses. A dog's nose gives him all the information he needs to put nutritional food in his body.

Dogs amaze me. When you are open to trusting your dogs, listening to your dogs and watching your dogs, you will start to see what I have seen over the years. As I said, dogs react. When a dog's behaviour changes, I pay attention.

On one occasion, I was walking a group of dogs off-leash along a canal. We had walked for about a kilometer when suddenly all the dogs came back and surrounded me. Immediately, I was looking around to see what was going on. I didn't notice anything, so I continued to walk. The dogs stayed close. Again, I stopped to look. To my surprise, there was a coyote across the canal in the field, quite difficult to see. I thought the coyote was acting oddly, so we started to head back to the car. All the dogs stayed close by, surrounding me. The coyote came up on the canal bank and followed us all the way back to the car before it ran off. I am not sure why the coyote followed us, but the dogs were uncomfortable and so we left. I was told later maybe she had pups. I will never know for sure, but I will always trust the dogs I know and love! They have given me many clues over the years.

I took a group of dogs out to a lake close to our home for an off-leash walk. I parked and let all the dogs out. I started to walk, and my dog Brady stayed behind. I continued to walk. Brady would not walk with us. If I continued to walk, he would take a few steps but not catch up with me. If I turned to walk back to him, he would turn and run back toward the car. He was acting strangely, trying to get my attention, so I headed back to him. I thought maybe he didn't feel well, but I really had no idea. He had never acted this way before. He loved going for off-leash walks with all his buddies. Before I even got back to the vehicle, one of the dogs came running to me. Her face was full of porcupine quills. Off to the vet we went. I believe Brady could smell the porcupine and tried his best to keep me and the other dogs away from the porcupines!

Recently, a friend told me her dog ran back to the vehicle and loaded up. This was very unusual for a dog that loved her off-leash runs. A couple of dogs had shown up on her walk. She normally would engage other dogs to play. She is a very playful dog, but she didn't want to play with these two dogs. I believe these two dogs had no interest in play, so she got herself into a safe spot.

Reba will walk closest to a person who has the weakest body language. Reba will walk close to me when others are stressed because their dogs won't listen. She will block a dog that runs right at me. Brady will correct any dog that tries to jump on me. Brady will stand behind me when he has had enough of a young pup, letting me know he needs my help to calm down this pup.

When the owner understands what they are doing to create the behaviour they dislike and applies simple solutions, problems can be easily resolved. The owner has to be willing to learn and understand dogs in order for change to happen.

It's my greatest wish that you learn something from what I have learned over the years. I am not a behaviourist, but I do understand dogs and I have many clients who would agree!

Take what you believe is of value for you and your new family member. Take action, be consistent and let your dog be a dog. They are amazing companion animals and deserve our respect.

www.ingramcontent.com/pod-product-compliance
Lightning Source LLC
Chambersburg PA
CBHW050438010526
44118CB00013B/1579